MW01245440

SUCCESS MNSTR™

SUCCESS MNSTR™
Conquering Unseen Challenges as You Strive to Reach Your Goals

Ashley Armstrong

Author photograph: Julia Burakova of Silver Moon Photography
Custom MNSTR glove: Bree-Anna Lehto, Emmy Award Winner Special FX Makeup Artist

Published by Game Changer Publishing

Paperback ISBN: 978-1-963793-78-9
Hardcover ISBN: 978-1-963793-79-6
Digital: ISBN: 978-1-963793-80-2

www.GameChangerPublishing.com

DISCLAIMER

This book is presented to you for informational purposes only and is not a substitute for any kind of professional or personal development advice. The content of this book is based solely on the personal views and opinions of the author, should not be considered scientific or correct conclusions, and do not represent the views of others. All information provided presented here is "as is" and without warranty of any kind, expressed or implied.

Although we strive to provide accurate general information in this book, we do not guarantee that the content is free from any errors or omissions, and you should not rely solely on this information. Always consult a professional in the area for your particular needs and circumstances prior to making any professional, business, legal, and financial or tax-related decisions.

The author of this book is not engaged in the practice of rendering any professional advice. You agree that under no circumstances, the author and/or our officers, employees, successors, shareholders, joint venture partners or anyone else working with the author shall be liable for any direct, indirect, incidental, consequential, equitable, special, punitive, exemplary or any other damages resulting from your use of this book including but not limited to all the content, information, stories and products presented here.

DEDICATION

To everyone striving to rise above the ordinary and embrace personal growth, this book is dedicated to you. May it serve as your guide to not only achieving MNSTR-level success but sustaining it in every aspect of your life.

ACKNOWLEDGMENTS

My life would be utterly incomplete without my incredible spouse, David. You are my rock, my greatest supporter, and the love of my life. You lift me up in every way, and I am beyond grateful to walk this journey with you. Together with our amazing children, Sage and Elaina, you are my world. Your love and support fuel my growth, driving me to push forward every day to give you the most beautiful life imaginable. Sage and Elaina, everything I do is for you—to give you the great life you deserve. I love you all more than words can say, and this book is truly for you… Thank you!

To my family—past and present—my grandmother (the matriarch), father (Super Dave), mother (intelligent athlete), sister (my first baby girl), aunts (second mothers), uncles (second fathers), cousins (cheerleaders), in-laws (all love-embracing), and extended family (the chosen ones): you are my tribe, my strength. You gave me the fire and the honor to chase my dreams, leave a legacy, embrace being different, and strive for the best. You are my everything.

To my coaches and friends, from childhood to today—your love and encouragement have shaped me in more ways than words can express. I'm deeply grateful to those who stood by me in my early years and to the cheerleaders who support me now. The lessons I've learned from each of you have guided me toward the person I will be tomorrow. I am forever thankful for your unwavering support and love. Thank you for being my foundation—I love you all so much!

To my professional family, who have walked with me on this incredible journey, I am profoundly grateful. Words can't fully capture the impact you've had on my life. Your unwavering support and belief in me have been invaluable as I've dared to dream and strived to help millions around the world. From the bottom of my heart, thank you to Dan Hollings, one of my biggest supporters, Tony Balistreri, Ian Jascourt, Elaine Wilkes, Daniel Hall, Anthony Hall, Mike Balmaceda, Drew Heriot, Matt Fisher, Sarah Sternberg, Roxy Stephenson, Stephen West, Tony Laidig, Kristen Laidig and my 'head' coach Hang Boge—you are all deeply loved and appreciated.

To Bree-Anna Lehto, my steadfast bestie, confidant, latte-therapist, and my connection to the real world—thank you for always being there, for understanding my quirks, and for creating my custom MNSTR glove. Your friendship means the world to me... You're basically my soulmate let's face it!

To those who have stepped up and rallied around me throughout the years, those who made a huge impact through just a few conversations, and those who've stood by me through thick and thin—you know who you are. I know I will miss many names in this list (please forgive me!), but know that I deeply respect and appreciate every one of you, no matter the role you've played in my life. I am so thankful and grateful for you!

Sarah Paikai, Jennifer Kem, Romy Signh, Katharine McMahon, Dave Cooper, John Anderson, Matt Harris, Izabela Hamilton, Rick Ornelas, Lambros Demos, Beth Nydick, Todd Herman, Chris Winfield, Jen Gottlieb, Alex Cattoni, Cameron Herold, Shamina Taylor, Robin

Joy Meyers, Nikole Mitchell, Norm Farrar, Menina D'Amours Fortunato, Maru Davila, Cari Kenzie, Chase Bowers, Brian Klecker, Michael Tranmer, Kayvon Kay, Seth Spears, Michael O'Neal, Clinton Senkow, Brad Malin, Deb Harrison, Zach Benson, Katya Varbanova, Amber Ybarra, Brittany Michalchuk, Forbes Riley, Colin Sprake, Neal S. Phalora, Tony Guarnaccia, Joseph D Lazukin, Steve Gosselin, Jennifer Sloan, Isabella Bedoya, Ron Reich, Alex Brown, JB Glossinger, Regina Peterburgsky, Amy Wees, Tatiana Tsoir, Joe Tolzmann, Betty Cardenas, Athena Severi, David Forward, Dave Armstrong, Jöelle Zee, Brent Armstrong, Karen Armstrong, Joan Armstrong, Menina D'Amours Fortunato, Kristen Elford-Pagé, David Forward Sr., Dan Faill, Skipp Skipperton, Kristen Marie, Katinka Bencs A., Amanda Webster, Sparky Bloodworth, Megan Carmack, Stacey Reid, Cindi Davidson Slawson, Alexsand Taylor, Tara Toews, Robin Joy Meyers, Hector Lopez M, Sherry Ryan, Steve Gardner, Jacobus Lavooij, Brad Malin, Kimberly Montano, Angela Marie Christian, Renee Williams, Dan Faill, Carol Montgomery, Lilianne Vargas, Angie Payne, Lisa Marie Ardagna, Donna Pickering, Asad Ali, Michelle Geisler Anderson, Becca Eve Young, Rick Loucks, Brent Armstrong, Misty Cates, Paige Peters, Bert Reid, Renee Fleming, Bernadette McDonnell, Cristian Von Hauser, Pam Proctor Chevalier, Benoit J. Pitts, Ellie Shoja, Cris Cawley, Nickie Savenetti Jarvies, Nicole Olazabal, Mike Mcginn, Selby Forward, Megan Hansell Henderson, Sue LaVigne, Carlene Leier, Menina D'Amours Fortunato, Ida Gustavson, Deborah Engerman, Wai Ling Gallagher, Nicola Peros Ballet Academy, Holly Waxman, Megan Carmack, Sherri Lynne Galbraith, Scott Miller, Katharine McMahon, Ashley Bowes Cash, Joshua Santana, Gail S. Norman, Deb Harrison, Jennifer Martin, Heather Farrell, Evan J. Cholfin, Natalee Allen Champlin, Monica Hershaft, Orlana Darkins Drewery, Robin Ann

Stoltman, Katia Hess, Sarah Sternberg, Chris Mcnaughton, Lilianne Vargas, Mallory Newton, Patrick Carleton, Adrian Loh, Dawn Stika, Wes Johnson, Sara Bronson, Cynthia Martinez, Mini America Park, Jennifer Knowles, Naomi Riley, Daniele G. Lattanzi, Carla Gitto, Raymond Mast, Ella Slawson, Naomi Riley, Michael York, Steven Thrasher, Ariana Bourke, Christina Flach, Adrian Loh, Heather Farrell, Joshua Santana, Scott Miller, Jason Barraclough, Ana Obee, Ali Farhat, Torque Bovay, Paul Barredo, Jason Scott, Marcy Reeves D'Alessandro, Au AnGels, Jacobus Lavooij, Anthony Franco, Manon Bolliger, Jane and Ted Brown, Adam and AJ Brown, Devil's Elbow racing crew, Victor Matthews, Auret Esselen, Jewel Tolentino, Keli Castineiras, Kat Elle, Joni Ross, Vlad, Jason Katzenback, Matt Clark, Nickie Jarvies, Jamie Smith, Kisma Orbovich, Kristalle Jime, Brett Kriger, Babe Mooney, Nicole McMullin, Ed and Nat Nijjer, Adrian Loh, Cary and Kristina Mullen, Dawn Stika, Jen Reichert, Asia and Damon Green, Tamara Carder, Kristy Verity, Brian Wright, Carlos Rodriguez, Otto Gail Corey Tyler Edlinger, Jim and Sue, Bobbi-Lynne McGarry, Jess Thomas, Corina Haensel, Grace Lee, Janis and Don Stevenson, Jamie Murphy, Michelle Blanchard, Nan May, Brandi Woodnutt, Breanna Crouse, Derek Pellizzari, Leeanne Fitzpatric, Lisa McGregor, Omar Aljebouri, Kristy Mitchell, Luke and Luke from the BeetleJuice group hahaha my Peterborough family, my Ski Racing family, my Lindsay family, my College family, my Whistler family, my Cabo family, my Vancouver family, and many, many more (I am missing so many)...

Read This First

Just to say thank you for buying and reading my book, I would like to email you a few free bonus gifts, no strings attached! Trust me, you'll want to claim your gift—I use mine every day!

To download your Free Gifts, scan the QR Code and bookmark the page; you'll return to it a few times while reading the book:

www.successmnstr.com/resources

SUCCESS MNSTR™

Conquering Unseen Challenges as You Strive to Reach Your Goals

Ashley Armstrong

www.GameChangerPublishing.com

Table of Contents

Introduction 1

Chapter 1 – The Duality of Being a Self-Creator...........................7

The Attraction of High Performance 9

Shadows at the Edge of the Limelight 12

Real-world High Achievers.. 16

Redefining the High Achiever's Journey 17

Summary 18

Chapter 2 – Bridging the Gap Between Generic Success Principles and Custom Strategies 21

My Personal Pinnacle of Achievement. . . & the Subsequent Abyss 23

The Birth of the Success MNSTR Archetypes a 29

Summary 31

Chapter 3 – The Success MNSTR Archetypes.............................33

Identify Your Archetype. . . Step #1....................................... 34

Athlete Archetype 35

Influencer Archetype.. 37

Scientist Archetype 39

Entrepreneur Archetype 41

Politician Archetype 42

Educated Archetype... 44

Public Advocate Archetype 46

Global Nomad Archetype 47

Monarch Archetype... 49

Summary 51

Chapter 4 – Rewiring for Success: The MNSTR Technique. . . Step #2.... 53

The Paradox of Success..58

The Need for a New Technique..65

Use It When You Need It...66

Summary..67

Chapter 5 – M Stands for Mindset 69

Growth-oriented Thinking 70

Benefits of a Growth Mindset..70

Ten Strategies for Cultivating a Growth Mindset 71

Summary..75

Chapter 6 – N Stands for Neurochemical Understanding........................ 77

Dopamine the Superstar Chemical 78

Neurochemical Imbalance and Its Impact.....................................81

Five Ways to Leverage Neurochemical Knowledge........................83

Summary..90

Chapter 7 – S Stands for Satisfaction (Intrinsic vs. Extrinsic) 91

Why Both Intrinsic and Extrinsic Sources of Motivation Matter..........92

The Interplay Between the Two..97

Cultivating Intrinsic Motivation in a World of Extrinsic Rewards 98

The Role of Societal Conditioning 99

Summary..99

Chapter 8 – T Stands for Treadmill Management 101

Five Tools to Escape the Hedonic Treadmill..................................103

The Happiness Baseline...106

Factors Influencing the Baseline..106

Boosting your Happiness Set Point...107

The 4 States of Happiness..108

Summary..111

Chapter 9 – R Stands for Restoration of Motivation and Wellness 113

    Fostering Well-Being for Lasting Peak Performance............................ 118

    Summary 121

Chapter 10 – The MNSTR Technique in Action 123

    Story #1: Uncharted Entrepreneur 125

    Story #2: Lily's Masterpieces.. 127

    Story #3: The Executive Rediscovering His Purpose.......................... 129

    Story #4: The Athlete's External Pressures 131

    Story #5: The Struggles of Self-Discovery..................................... 133

    Story #6: Barely Breathing to Fully Alive (My Story).......................... 136

    Summary.. 143

Chapter 11 – Harnessing your MNSTR: The Power Within................... 145

    Defining your cheerleader 146

    Leveraging your cheerleader.. 146

    Ignoring External Noise.. 147

    Fuel for your fire 149

    Summary 150

Chapter 12 – Navigating Your Cycles of Sabotage or Comfort 151

    Taking the Success Paradox Self-Assessment 152

    Summary 154

Final Thoughts 157

References.. 163

Introduction

Success:
We covet it, chase it, and celebrate it.
It's often seen as the ultimate prize for all the hard
work we do in pursuit of our endeavors.

But does success truly provide a sense of fulfillment and
happiness, or does it disguise a more complex reality?

You know, it's interesting...

I've had countless conversations with people who view me as an expert in success dynamics, yet many of them don't feel truly successful. These are individuals who identify as self-starters, self-creators, self-motivators, or high achievers, yet they struggle to match their own accomplishments with society's narrow expectations of success. But let's pause for a moment—what does it really mean to be successful?

There's a belief, almost a myth, that you can only understand success once you've already "made it." Many assume you must be at the top of your game—wealthy, polished, an icon of authority—to even grasp what success is. Or worse, that you don't need to understand success until you've reached it. It's like saying, "I'll learn to raise a child after they're born," or, "I'll figure out retirement when it's time to retire." Waiting to learn about success after you've achieved it is not just backward, it's risky.

Success isn't exclusive to those with the highest incomes or prestigious titles. It's about those who push through obstacles, who go further than those content with merely getting by. These aren't people with magical talents or secret formulas—they're just stubborn enough to keep going when others stop.

That's why protecting what you've already worked for and defining your own relationship with success needs to start now—not after some arbitrary milestone is met. Waiting until you've "become successful" may be too late. I know this firsthand.

I didn't fully understand the weight of success until I achieved something so monumental, so daunting, that it nearly shattered me. We all dream big, thinking, "Why not strive for something great?" But the days pass whether you act or not, and sometimes, success sneaks up on you.

When I hit this milestone, it felt like being struck by a semi-truck. At first, it was exhilarating—overwhelmingly so. But quickly, it turned into my worst nightmare. I finally understood why some ambitious individuals hold back, fearful of what success might demand: the new rules, the expectations, the hard-earned lessons. Upleveling your life takes more than just desire—it demands energy, time, and relentless commitment. Often, the fear of success itself becomes paralyzing, especially when you're already running on empty.

Looking back, I realize that when success catches you off guard, it's like a rollercoaster you can't get off. And, for me, I almost derailed completely.

What is Success?

Success, in all its forms, is a universal aspiration. It's deeply embedded in the human psyche, driving us to push boundaries, explore new horizons, and constantly raise the bar. This relentless pursuit has fueled some of humanity's greatest achievements, pushing us toward brighter futures.

Yet, like the most captivating stories, the journey to success is full of unexpected twists. Those who reach the pinnacle of their goals often confront challenges that are unique, complex, and paradoxical—obstacles they never anticipated.

The view from the top, while exhilarating, can be disorienting and even lonely.

The thrill of achievement often fades,
leaving a haunting question:
"Now what?"

The pressure to stay on top, innovate, and meet ever-increasing expectations can become overwhelming. Success doesn't just change your circumstances—it can change you. There's the constant tension between who you were before the accolades and who you've become in the spotlight.

In this book, we'll explore the intricate world of achievement. We'll dive into the minds of self-starters and high achievers, uncover what truly drives them, and offer a roadmap for navigating the often tumultuous journey toward reaching your greatest goals.

The Success MNSTR™ methodology guides individuals through a **two-part process**: first, identifying your Success MNSTR Archetype (your inner critic) to discover who you truly are...

and then applying the five key elements of the MNSTR Technique™ to help you move forward:

M MINDSET

N NEUROCHEMICAL UNDERSTANDING

S SATISFACTION (INTRINSIC VS. EXTRINSIC)

T TREADMILL MANAGEMENT (HEDONIC)

R RESTORATION OF MOTIVATION & WELLNESS

Together, they offer a personalized approach for high achievers. First, individuals identify their unique persona and operational style, then the Technique helps them uncover strategies, insights, and tools to not just succeed but thrive sustainably—right in the moment, in real-time. You can even use the accompanying workbook to track your progress and epiphanies. This holistic approach empowers individuals to navigate life's highs and lows, ensuring progress and fulfillment tailored specifically to high achievers.

The journey ahead is not only relevant to those who strive for success, but it also sheds light on universal human experiences, providing valuable lessons and opportunities for reflection. My goal is to destigmatize the post-success blues, much like how society has begun to address postpartum depression after giving birth. Whether you see yourself as a high achiever, aspire to be one, or are simply fascinated by the complexities of success, the wisdom in these pages is here for you.

Welcome to the paradox of success. Let's begin!

CHAPTER 1

The Duality of Being a Self-Creator
What Characteristics Set a High Achiever Apart?

In every industry and discipline—such as boardrooms to athletic fields, art studios, and research labs—We find exceptional individuals known as go-getters, self-creators, self-motivators, self-starters, or high achievers. I'll use "high achiever" as the term to encompass them all throughout the book.

High achievers don't just meet standards; they continuously redefine them. Because their abilities can be observed everywhere, it's essential to note that being a high achiever isn't just about amassing wealth or accolades. It's about pushing limits and embracing challenges that others find insurmountable, whether that means graduating from school, initiating a business venture, losing weight, running a marathon, climbing the corporate ladder, becoming a caregiver, or mastering a new skill. Here are some hallmark characteristics and practices of high achievers.

Resilience in the face of Adversity
UNYIELDING PASSION
Proactive Mindset   *GOAL-ORIENTED APPROACHES*
Unquenchable Thirst for Knowledge

Unyielding Passion

High achievers often possess a burning passion for their chosen fields and endeavors. This isn't a fleeting interest but a deep-seated commitment that fuels their journey, rain or shine.

Goal-oriented Approaches

While many of us regularly set goals, high achievers display an uncanny ability to identify ambitious yet achievable targets. They outline meticulous strategies and relentlessly pursue these goals with laser-like focus.

Resilience in the Face of Adversity

Setbacks are inevitable, but high achievers view them as stepping stones rather than roadblocks. Their resilience enables them to bounce back from failures and emerge stronger and more determined to keep moving forward.

Unquenchable Thirst for Knowledge

Complacency isn't in a high achiever's vocabulary. They constantly seek new ways to expand their horizons and refine their skills.

Proactive Mindset

Instead of waiting for opportunities to present themselves, high achievers create them. They're proactive, taking initiative and often charting paths where none previously existed.

The Attraction of High Performance

Society's admiration for high achievers isn't coincidental. We are innately drawn to the extraordinary—the ones who redefine limits. Their achievements not only stand as testaments to human capabilities, but also inspire countless others. Shattered records, unprecedented solutions, an artistic piece moving an entire generation: these moments don't just earn a person their accolades.

SHARE WISDOM AND INSPIRE OTHERS
Create a Legacy   PERSONAL GROWTH
FUN   Recognition and Respect
Financial Freedom   Hiring Help
SCHEDULE
Philanthropy   Personal Fulfillment
Opportunities Galore

Recognition and Respect

Accomplishments earn high achievers admiration, recognition, and respect from peers, mentors, and even competitors.

Personal Fulfillment

Achieving their goals brings immense satisfaction and a sense of purpose.

Opportunities Galore

Glowing track records open doors to new opportunities, partnerships, and ventures.

Financial Freedom

Financial stability provides freedom from the worries that inevitably come with bills and unexpected expenses.

Philanthropy

Thanks to financial success, they're able to give to causes or people in need, or even startups they believe in, and experience the joy of making a difference and even transforming lives.

Schedule

Opportunities and financial stability mean they act on their own terms, unbounded by anyone else's schedule. They can come and go as they please.

FUN

Indulging in fun activities is made possible by their time management, allowing them to enjoy recreational pursuits and create lasting memories.

Hiring Help

They can hire individuals for tasks such as bookkeeping, cleaning, organizing, meal delivery, personal training, and therapy, which leaves more time for fun and philanthropy.

Create a Legacy

They lay foundations for future generations to build on in their respective fields and pursuits.

Share Wisdom and Inspire Others

They share their stories, offering guidance to others on similar journeys. Their successes inspire others to pursue their own dreams.

Personal Growth

With time and resources, they can invest in their own personal development as well as that of others. They understand the adage, "It's lonely at the top, but it's so crowded at the bottom."

However, the luminosity of success also casts some shadows, which can turn the high achiever's journey into a double-edged sword.

Shadows at the Edge of the Limelight

Shadows lurk behind the glistening facade of achievements. The relentless spotlight brings with it immense pressure and suffocating expectations. The mental and emotional strain of sustaining that "golden" status, becoming a target, coupled with the fear of losing it, can sometimes be more challenging than the actual path that gets one there.

Changes to Relationships   **Mindset**   *Boredom*

Guilt   Jealousy

Safety Concerns

Identity Crisis   MANAGING MONEY

Trust Issues

THE WEIGHT OF EXPECTATIONS

JUDGMENT FROM PEERS   TEMPTATION

Financial Requests   **Burnout**

Unworthiness   Loneliness at the top

The Weight of Expectations

With each success, they're confronted with a higher bar. The pressure to outperform themselves, surpass past achievements, and meet escalating expectations can weigh heavily on them. They may even start to wonder if they're just a one-hit wonder.

Loneliness at the Top

The journey to success can be isolating. They might feel misunderstood or even distanced from their peers.

Burnout

Relentless drive and commitment can lead to both physical and mental exhaustion, pushing them to their limits.

Identity Crisis

Their achievements may become so fused with their identity that any setback feels intensely personal and can spark self-doubt and questions about their purpose.

Guilt

They might grapple with the disparity between their own progress, wealth, and success, and that of others.

Unworthiness

Feelings of unworthiness can creep in, casting doubt on one's accomplishments. Despite external validation, individuals may struggle internally with feelings of inadequacy or imposter syndrome. These doubts can undermine confidence and hinder further progress, leading to a perpetual cycle of self-doubt.

Jealousy

Some might envy their achievements, which can lead to strained relationships.

Judgment from Peers

Sharing their successes can cause varied reactions. They might face different degrees of judgment from those who scrutinize their outward signs of success.

Safety Concerns

Their status might make them the target of scams, theft, or even more severe threats.

Trust Issues

Discerning who to trust becomes more challenging as jealousy and negativity from others become more common.

Mindset

Without adopting an abundance mindset, they might squander their success without forethought.

Changes to Relationships

It can become challenging to discern if some relationships are genuine, or if they're more motivated by their success, connections, or wealth.

Temptation

With success, the ability to access and acquire the finer things increases, as does the risk of overindulgence and impulsive decisions.

Boredom

Success often brings the challenge of replicating the process that led to it. While they may have achieved success once, the meticulous steps to recreate it may not be fully understood or appreciated. This familiarity can breed boredom, leading individuals to seek out new, more exciting ventures instead of repeating a known process.

Financial Requests

They might encounter requests or demands for financial help from friends or family members.

Managing Money

Increased wealth often brings the stress of managing it effectively, including filing one's taxes correctly, making sound investments, and wealth preservation.

Real-world High Achievers

History is crowded with tales of luminaries who, following their monumental achievements, grappled with unforeseen challenges. Michael Phelps, triumphant at the Olympics, went on to battle post-success blues. Elon Musk faced a serious void after a billion-dollar exit. Artists like Adele struggle to recreate the magic of a chart-topping hit. Writers like Elizabeth Gilbert might lose themselves after their books turn into box-office hits. These stories, though different, share a common theme: the paradox of high achievement. You get exactly what you wanted but realize it doesn't make you happy or fulfill you as expected. It's truly a double-edged sword.

Paradox of high achievement

When it comes to understanding the world of high achievers, it's crucial to include this duality in our analysis. The journey is a blend of exhilarating highs and challenging lows, and by acknowledging both the privileges and pressures, we pave the way for a more holistic, empathetic, and constructive dialogue on success.

Redefining the High Achiever's Journey

While the aforementioned markers of success are valid, they often only skim the surface of the concept and fail to capture the depths and nuances of a high achiever's journey.

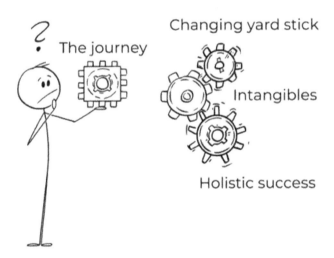

The Intangibles

High achievers don't just chase tangible outcomes; they also seek intangible rewards like personal growth, self-awareness, and the joy that can be derived from the process itself. These intrinsic values often hold more weight than any external accolade. Aside from general admiration, high achievers often enjoy both tangible benefits (trips, dinners, shopping, concerts, VIP treatment, and monetary rewards) and intangibles (self-love, respect, influence, and a lasting legacy).

Focus More on the Journey and Less on the Destination

For many high achievers, success isn't a single destination, but a continuous journey with many landmarks. The traditional outlook on success might celebrate the main outcome while overlooking the grit, persistence, failures, and insight that paved the way.

The Changing Yardstick

What constitutes success is a constantly evolving idea to high achievers. Once they attain a goal, they set benchmarks for a new one. Because of this, society's more static definitions might not be able to keep pace with their dynamic aspirations.

Holistic, Authentic Success

High achievers often view success in terms of how it encompasses one's mental and physical well-being, meaningful relationships, and an authentic sense of purpose. This broad spectrum extends beyond the narrow confines of societal definitions.

Summary

High achievers continually redefine success, focusing on the rich experiences, aspirations, and setbacks that shape their journey. Modern society's metrics of success—wealth and recognition—often miss these deeper personal narratives. To truly understand a high achiever's world, we must look beyond surface-level definitions and appreciate the full spectrum of experiences. Success is about evolving, learning, and thriving, not merely about reaching goals or accumulating acco-lades. Holistic success involves personal growth, self-awareness, and balancing the journey with tangible outcomes.

3 Key Takeaways:

1. High Achievers Redefine Limits: They push boundaries be-yond societal standards, driven by passion and a goal-oriented mindset.

2. Shadows of Success: High achievers face pressures like burn-out, loneliness, and self-doubt despite outward success.

3. Holistic Success Matters: True success isn't just external achievements—it includes personal growth, mental well-being, and a focus on the journey.

CHAPTER 2

Bridging the Gap Between Generic Success Principles and Custom Strategies

Success is Not a "One Size Fits All" Model

Generic success principles provide a broad foundation, offering tools and guidelines that can help individuals pursue personal and professional growth. From time management techniques to motivational quotes, they serve as roadmaps for achievement.

One size does not fit all!

However, high achievers—whether graduating from school, learning a new skill, earning a license, starting a business, or excelling in their career—operate in a realm defined by lofty ambitions and unique setbacks. These individuals need more than basic strategies; they require advanced tools tailored to their specific challenges and aspirations, where conventional advice might fall short.

For example, high achievers might confront deeper questions like:

- "Was it just luck?"
- "Are they going to find out I am a fraud?"
- "Do I really need to keep putting myself out there?"
- "Why am I scared when I've done this before?"
- "How can I keep going without burning out?"
- "What if someone outdoes me and I lose my place in the spotlight?"
- "How can I enjoy the process, not just the goal?"
- "Do I really have to go through this all over again to stay successful?"
- "How can I keep going when I just want to give up?"
- "Is it okay to dream of being an employee to avoid entrepreneur stress?"
- "How can I succeed again if I don't know how I did it the first time?"
- "Am I afraid of success because of what it will take for me to achieve it?"
- "Now what?"

My Personal Pinnacle of Achievement. . . and the Subsequent Abyss

I pushed myself to the limit to succeed!

I was born into a pro-athletic family where excellence was a multi-generational legacy. My father, an exceptional multi-sport pro-athlete, alpine ski racing coach, and inventor, spent over 40 years working with top athletes in the snow sport industry. He worked with legendary athletes like the Crazy Canucks—Dave Irwin, Dave Murray, Steve Podborski, Jim Hunter, and Ken Read—as well as Olympic champions like Cary Mullen and Brian Stemmle, to name just a few. Growing up in this environment of high achievers, I always felt immense pressure to stand atop the podium. The rule was simple: "If you aren't hurt, you aren't trying hard enough."

This background was both a blessing and a burden. It gave me the confidence to bet on myself from a young age, excelling in every sport.

Academically, though, I struggled. Diagnosed with learning disabilities, I spent my school years separated in a small room with other students facing learning challenges. Learning that I couldn't go to college due to not meeting the general education level was a huge blow. It was an embarrassment I wore like a mark of disgrace, but failure wasn't an option. I wasn't willing to accept that. I spent my final high school years doing everything possible to qualify—attending summer school and even returning to high school after graduation.

My sports background gave me the courage and dedication to keep fighting. From elementary school to college, the snow sports industry became my sanctuary. I fully stepped into my father's shadow, feeling even more pressure to succeed. I competed, coached, started racing schools, and earned a degree in ski resort operations. Looking back, I was a natural-born athlete—it's in the blood. But despite that talent, I didn't have the Olympic heart my father admired in others.

Determined to prove myself once again, I moved across the country, then to a foreign land where I didn't speak the language. I launched several ventures, becoming a natural health practitioner and brewing probiotic hangover tonics for locals and tourists. After becoming a mother to two girls, I wrote six best-selling children's books about life lessons for them in case I passed away early. As a community leader and childbirth educator, I founded a mothers' group that continues to thrive 13 years later. I found success in manufacturing and consulting, only to face setbacks—inventory issues, copycats, con artists, and bad partnerships. These challenges ultimately led me to pivot to TV, where I reached millions as a guest expert during the COVID crisis, even though I couldn't save my own business.

I could never escape my father's shadow. My relentless work ethic and need for recognition drove me to exhaustion. Each business venture felt inadequate, despite continuing to hit "success" milestones. Eventually, I joined a partnership in an unfamiliar industry after months of persuasion.

The creation of this book comes from the personal crash that followed achieving the pinnacle of my professional dreams in that partnership: the largest worldwide digital marketing launch, making $57 million in the first seven months and closing the year at $70 million. I stood at the pinnacle of success and remember proclaiming, "I can die happy tomorrow because I've accomplished everything I've ever wanted up to this point."

This was my moment to make my dad proud and prove everyone wrong!

Yet, after reaching the top, the void I felt was profound. I wrestled with whether to share this accomplishment with even my closest friends and family, unsure of how they would react. A friend had faced similar challenges after purchasing a luxury car following a financial milestone. His relationships shifted—jealousy surfaced and expectations grew—turning the joy of success into a burden. Eventually, the stress outweighed the happiness, and he sold the car, leaving me to question if sharing my own success was worth it.

As awards and money poured in, I realized I wasn't prepared for what followed; this success didn't replicate itself immediately, so it started to feel like a one-hit-wonder. The sudden wealth, though life-changing for many, didn't bring the positive changes I had anticipated. Managing money, making significant financial decisions, and grappling with heavy taxes made my hard-earned rewards feel elusive. The government had a firm grasp on what they deemed their share, and I struggled to find effective professional assistance. I began worrying about the future and whether I had already reached my peak.

I had given up my own business ventures at this point and was relying solely on the partnership for income. Fear of losing it left me anxious, driving me to work more, and spend less time focused on my family and my children's well-being. They struggled at school—poor grades, bullying, and social isolation—causing deep depression. This stress carried over to my spouse too, who did his best to support me and the kids, while feeling his own pressures to compensate financially because of my uncertain income.

As we focused on stabilizing our income, we inadvertently neglected our children, who paid the highest price. This struggle didn't just affect my role as a business partner—it robbed me of the ability to be there for my children when they needed me most. I couldn't give them the emotional support or love they craved—the kind of love children understand as "TIME." Even worse, I neglected my spouse—the one person who had stood by me for 20 years. I am who I am (in life) today because of him. He always called me his best investment, but I doubt he felt that way anymore.

And as for my well-being? It didn't just take a back seat—it was practically left behind entirely!

As parents, we are expected to be the pillars of stability for our family, and when we fall short, it feels like a profound failure. This relentless pressure pushed me to my breaking point, leading me to question the very purpose of my existence. At my lowest moments, I even believed my family might be better off without me, as I struggled to replicate the success and financial stability I thought they needed.

Days blurred into months as I battled through paralyzing and debilitating panic attacks, often finding myself unable to get out of bed or curled up in fetal positions in the middle of the room, contemplating whether to call 911. Hidden tears were a constant companion during work calls, as I tried to conceal the compounding truth of my profound sense of despair. Overwhelming self-doubt gripped me like a vice, leaving me physically and mentally exhausted. My jaw clenched so tightly that I wore a mouth guard while working to protect my teeth. However, the constant clenching made eating painful, forcing me to rely on a mostly liquid diet. Stress took a visible toll on my body—my hair started falling out, my joints stiffened, and wrinkles seemed to appear overnight, making me feel as though I was aging prematurely.

I was consumed by anger, lashing out, screaming, and yelling daily, desperate for help managing the family. In a desperate attempt to cope, I turned to smoking again, finding temporary relief in the haze of addiction. At home, I was a failure; while at work, I maintained a facade of composure as best as possible. The weight of responsibilities pressed heavily on my shoulders, leaving me feeling crushed under the burden.

This wasn't merely a phase of low spirits; it was a year-long spiral during which I lacked direction, meaning, and purpose. The absence of my own means of making money outside my partnership and a clear next goal intensified the torment, and the control I once had over my life slipped from my grasp. In my darkest hours, I found myself entertaining thoughts of ending it all.

It was like I had birthed this immense success, only to be struck with a wicked case of postpartum depression.

One of the hardest aspects of this journey was grappling with the disconnect between my mind and heart. Logically, I knew I had achieved something remarkable. I had so much to be grateful for, and my life was worth celebrating. Yet, my inner critic—I call it the Success MNSTR—twisted my thoughts and emotions, leaving me feeling isolated and confused. It was a lonely paradox. Who could I confide in? Who would even understand the emotional complexity of achieving something so great, only to feel so lost?

Conversations with my sister helped me see a pattern: I had been carrying this Success MNSTR for a long time. Competing in sports, school, living abroad, entrepreneurship, and motherhood—all followed the same highs and lows. I realized success had imposed relentless expectations, raising questions of identity, reinvention, and how to continually prove myself. The real challenge wasn't just finding a new passion but surpassing past achievements—a never-ending cycle.

Even with this realization of my pattern, this was a challenging time. New ideas sparked excitement, each seeming to promise another adrenaline rush in the pursuit of my next *magnum opus*. Resisting the temptation to chase yet another professional milestone was difficult, as it mirrored my lifelong search for purpose, identity, and self-worth. The fear of never reaching such heights again gnawed at me. I felt trapped, but also like I was floating in limbo with nothing to keep me grounded, spinning and spinning. My mind was a blur, devoid of motivation like an unprimed canvas, unwilling to accept paint.

Each day, I wondered how to begin again. As I contemplated that very question, along with so many others, the Success MNSTR Archetypes and the MNSTR Technique emerged from the ashes, just like a phoenix.

The Birth of the Success MNSTR Archetypes and the MNSTR Technique

The realization that I was stuck in an endless cycle of chasing success was a turning point for me. Every goal I accomplished came with the pressure to do something bigger, faster, and better. The fear of never reaching such heights again haunted me, and I was caught between wanting to shift my focus to a new purpose and struggling with the constant demand to prove myself.

This wasn't just a phase—it was a deeply ingrained pattern in my life. My identity had become so closely tied to my accomplishments that without a new goal to chase, I felt lost, unworthy, and unfulfilled. I wasn't just a high achiever; I had let my Success MNSTR dictate my every move. But success doesn't have to define who you are. It's only one piece of the puzzle, and it doesn't have to consume you.

From this time of introspection—and diving into neuroscience, psychology, and personality traits—I uncovered unique personas, which led to the creation of the 9 Success MNSTR Archetypes. But understanding myself wasn't enough. I needed a real-time, actionable system to help me course-correct and keep moving forward whenever my Success MNSTR decided to show up. That's how the MNSTR Technique was born—a structured method designed to help me and other high achievers navigate their paths without veering off track.

The MNSTR Technique helped me understand this pattern and, more importantly, take control of it. It taught me how to navigate the highs and lows of achievement without getting lost in them, recognize when I was feeding the wrong side of my Success MNSTR, and consciously shift my mindset to break the cycle of burnout and frustration.

By managing my Success MNSTR, I found clarity and purpose beyond just checking off goals. True satisfaction comes not from constantly proving yourself to others but from understanding who you are, what you value, and how you want to live your life—without the constant pressure of chasing the next big thing.

This journey hasn't been easy, but it's been transformative. I've learned that success isn't about how fast you can climb the mountain—it's about enjoying the view from each step along the way. With this understanding, I've been able to redefine success, find peace in the present moment, and regain control over my life, mind, and happiness.

The Success MNSTR Technique is now my guide, my compass. It reminds me that I'm more than just my achievements. And with these tools, I hope to help others realize they are too. Understanding how to harness this power begins by identifying your unique archetype. In the next chapter, we'll explore all 9 Success MNSTR Archetypes—distinct personas that reveal key aspects of your drive, patterns, and the shadow side that influence your success. By recognizing your archetype, you'll gain clarity on how to move forward with purpose and focus.

Summary

This chapter delves into the realization that success is not just about constant achievement but managing the emotional patterns that follow it. I share through my own journey how I was able to identify this pattern, which led to the creation of the 9 Success MNSTR Archetypes and the MNSTR Technique, which provide personalized strategies for high achievers to navigate the highs and lows of success without losing themselves.

3 Key Takeaways:

1. There's plenty of advice on achieving success, but little on managing it once you've arrived. Coping with the emotional impact requires personalized strategies based on your archetype to handle the aftermath.

2. Emotional challenges like exhaustion and self-doubt often accompany high achievement.

3. Managing these challenges with tailored strategies helps high achievers maintain motivation, clarity, and well-being throughout their journey.

CHAPTER 3

The Success MNSTR Archetypes

Lighting the Way for High Achievers... **Step #1**

The Success MNSTR Archetypes provide ambitious individuals with transformative insights into their identity, revealing different aspects of the high achiever's journey.

Step #1 in mastering your success is identifying your own MNSTR Archetype. Naming your MNSTR sparks a unique neurological response, forming a personal connection that strengthens your relationship with it. Document your archetype and takeaways in the Success MNSTR Workbook. Understanding your archetype builds resilience and self-awareness, revealing strengths, passions, and obstacles. Managing your MNSTR unlocks true success, fueling growth rather than draining energy.

Identify Your Archetype

If you haven't taken it yet, the Success MNSTR Archetype quiz will help you discover your MNSTR, and it only takes about 5 minutes. Don't overthink the questions—just read through and pick the answer that feels best in the moment. The quiz is designed to reveal your archetype, and it might not fully make sense until the end. Trust the process—don't overanalyze; the truth will show in the result.

To take the quiz, head to the free gift resource page you accessed by scanning the QR code at the beginning of the book, checking your email, or simply re-scan the code with your phone now.

www.successmnstr.com/resources

The results you'll receive after taking the quiz are packed with insights to help you align your aspirations, goals, and values. Please share your MNSTR with me by using **#SuccessMNSTR** on any social media platform.

Next, I'll introduce you to all nine distinct archetype personas. However, remember that each has a more in-depth explanation in your quiz results. As you review them, keep in mind these examples are just a glimpse, meant to inspire you.

Athlete Archetype

What motivates this Success MNSTR Archetype persona?

The Athlete is driven by a profound passion for excelling in their chosen field. Also fueled by the exhilaration of competition, the pursuit of victory, and the thirst for recognition and admiration, they have the urge to consistently outperform in order to secure their place as the best of the best.

What supportive strengths, habits, and behaviors does this Success MNSTR Archetype persona have?

The Athlete personifies discipline, perseverance, determination, and resilience. A strong work ethic helps them maintain a rigorous training regimen, and they are ardently goal-oriented. Physical well-being is paramount because it ensures peak performance. Their demeanor exudes sportsmanship, and they inspire others with their unwavering spirit of teamwork.

What is the sabotaging dark side of this Success MNSTR Archetype persona?

The Athlete's shadows emerge as unforgiving self-criticism, an unhealthy obsession with perfection, their susceptibility to burnout, and an incessant need to win. Their fear of failure can lead to self-imposed pressure and a debilitating habit of continuously validating their prowess.

The Treadmill Trap

Continuously seeking the next pinnacle of success, they may feel perpetually unsatisfied, neglecting to recognize or relish in their current and latest achievements. The never-ending quest for the next win can make them feel like they're always running in place.

Who fits this Archetype?

Meet James, a top executive at a marketing firm who thrives on out-pacing competition and hitting targets. His intense discipline and relentless drive have earned him professional admiration. Yet, behind every success, James battles constant self-criticism and the pressure to outperform. He rarely stops to celebrate his wins, instead pushing immediately toward the next goal. Trapped on the treadmill of achievement, James is always chasing the next victory, never truly satisfied.

Influencer Archetype

What motivates this Success MNSTR Archetype persona?

The Influencer seeks popularity, recognition, and validation from their perceived audience. They are driven by positive feedback, a growing fan base, and their aspiration to be celebrated and influential in their respective fields.

What supportive strengths, habits, and behaviors does this Success MNSTR Archetype persona have?

They possess natural charisma and the ability to engage and captivate their audience. Expertise in self-promotion, networking, and personal branding, as well as resilience, and effective communication define them. Their adaptability and creativity, coupled with the ability to leverage collaborations, amplify their influence.

What is the sabotaging dark side of this Success MNSTR Archetype persona?

They may excessively seek external validation, becoming overly reliant on popularity metrics. The pressure to curate a perfect public image and negative feedback can strain their mental health and authenticity.

The Treadmill Trap

The continuous chase for more likes, followers, and recognition can lead to exhaustion. As trends change, the pressure to stay relevant can make them feel as if they are always in motion but never truly moving forward.

Who fits this Archetype?

Meet Mia, a public relations manager who thrives on connecting with others and building her brand. Known for her charisma and ability to engage, she has a knack for creating connections that expand her influence. Mia's motivation comes from positive feedback and the desire to be seen as a thought leader. However, she often finds herself overrelying on external validation, constantly chasing likes and recognition. The pressure to maintain a perfect image can leave her feeling drained and stuck in an endless loop of seeking approval.

Scientist Archetype

What motivates this Success MNSTR Archetype persona?

The Scientist is driven by the pursuit of knowledge, advancements in their field, and recognition from peers and industry leaders for their groundbreaking work. Their motivation stems from solving complex problems and discovering new information. Notably, the Scientist excels in maintaining emotional detachment, allowing them to approach challenges with clarity and focus, unfettered by personal biases or distractions.

What supportive strengths, habits, and behaviors does this Success MNSTR Archetype persona have?

Scientists bring meticulous research skills, disciplined analyses, critical thinking, and a strong sense of curiosity to their work. They value collaboration and feedback, and challenge existing paradigms so as to always aim for accuracy and continuous learning.

What is the sabotaging dark side of this Success MNSTR Archetype persona?

The Scientist may grapple with fears of being proven incorrect, is prone to overemphasizing past failures, and tends to fixate on perfectionism. This can lead to self-doubt and even stagnation in their progress. However, their analytical nature sometimes obscures the emotional side of their experiences, making it challenging for them to connect deeply with their own feelings or those of others.

The Treadmill Trap

Scientists, in their pursuit of both validation and knowledge, can become trapped in a cycle of seeking constant recognition, leading to complacency and risk avoidance. This might prevent them from truly innovating or venturing into the unknown territory of their field.

Who fits this Archetype?

Meet Alex, a software engineer driven by the pursuit of innovation and knowledge. Known for his critical thinking and problem-solving skills, Alex spends hours fine-tuning code, always seeking to push the boundaries of technology. His motivation comes from the thrill of discovery and recognition from peers. However, his fixation on perfection sometimes leads to self-doubt and stagnation. Struggling with the fear of being wrong, Alex can find himself trapped in the need for validation, avoiding risk and stifling creativity.

Entrepreneur Archetype

What motivates this Success MNSTR Archetype persona?

Entrepreneurs are driven by the desire for financial control, autonomy, and the freedom to create a lifestyle that reflects their values. They are passionate about exploring new ideas and making a significant, positive impact on others.

What supportive strengths, habits, and behaviors does this Success MNSTR Archetype persona have?

Entrepreneurs possess financial acumen and a passion for innovation, and they value independence. Their habits include continuous learning and taking calculated risks. They are proactive, efficient networkers, and consistently display a commendable work ethic.

What is the sabotaging dark side of this Success MNSTR Archetype persona?

Entrepreneurs might grapple with self-doubt, especially when the results of their endeavors don't align with their previous expectations. They may constantly compare themselves to others and can experience burnout when they neglect self-care practices in favor of their intense pursuit of success.

The Treadmill Trap

Entrepreneurs can sometimes get caught in a cycle of relentlessly pursuing financial success and innovation. This constant chase can lead them to overlook the importance of balance, resulting in emotional and physical fatigue.

Who fits this Archetype?

Meet Levi, the founder of a thriving e-commerce startup. He's driven by innovation and values the freedom of running his own business, creating a company that aligns with his core beliefs. Levi's ambition for financial independence keeps him constantly learning, networking, and embracing calculated risks. However, the pressure to succeed often leaves him feeling burned out and filled with self-doubt, particularly when he compares himself to others. Levi frequently struggles with balance, prioritizing work over self-care as he chases his next big breakthrough.

Politician Archetype

POLITICIAN

What motivates this Success MNSTR Archetype persona?

Politicians are driven by the need for approval, endorsement, and validation from others. They prioritize decisions that will gain them the acceptance of their constituents and tend to focus on being perceived as likable and politically correct.

What supportive strengths, habits, and behaviors does this Success MNSTR Archetype persona have?

Politicians possess effective communication skills and a working knowledge of diplomacy and building symbiotic relationships. They excel at engaging with diverse opinions, negotiating compromises, and navigating complex arenas. Their habits include active listening, strategic decision-making, and cultivating a favorable public image.

What is the sabotaging dark side of this Success MNSTR Archetype persona?

Politicians often struggle with the temptation to prioritize popularity over personal values or party objectives over personal convictions and may sometimes come across as hypocrites. They also find it challenging to reconcile their public persona with their authentic self, which often leads to forced conformity rather than genuine self-expression.

The Treadmill Trap

In their desire to serve the greater good and leave a lasting legacy, Politicians can get tangled up in the constant balancing act of maintaining their public image versus embracing personal authenticity. The continuous effort to gain and maintain approval, thereby avoiding rejection, can sometimes overshadow their true self and core values.

Who fits this Archetype?

Meet Aisha, the head of her company's marketing team, who thrives on building strong relationships and being liked by colleagues. Her excellent communication skills and ability to mediate diverse opinions make her a natural leader. However, Aisha often struggles with prioritizing popularity over her true values, sometimes conforming to fit others' expectations. The constant pressure to maintain a flawless image can overshadow her authentic self, leaving her trapped in the pursuit of approval while sacrificing her personal convictions.

Educated Archetype

What motivates this Success MNSTR Archetype persona?

The Educated persona is deeply motivated by the quest for knowledge and intellectual development. They find satisfaction in mastering complex subjects and acquiring degrees or certifications and desire recognition for their contributions.

What supportive strengths, habits, and behaviors does this Success MNSTR Archetype persona have?

They are characterized by their extensive repositories of knowledge, an unwavering commitment to education and their studies, and insightful and informed opinions. Their strengths lie in research, analysis, and critical thinking, making them valuable resources for their expertise and fresh perspectives.

What is the sabotaging dark side of this Success MNSTR Archetype persona?

Challenges faced by the Educated include a tendency to overthink, sometimes excessive self-doubt, and potential elitist behavior. All of these attributes can alienate them from those who may not share the same level of academic or intellectual achievement.

The Treadmill Trap

The Educated may get ensnared in an endless cycle of acquiring degrees and certifications, mistaking theoretical knowledge for true wisdom. The quest for constant validation might even begin to overshadow the importance of practical application.

Who fits this Archetype?

Meet Emily, a research analyst who thrives on expanding her knowledge and mastering complex topics. She's constantly seeking intellectual growth through courses, certifications, and in-depth research, finding satisfaction in being recognized for her expertise. However, her drive to acquire more knowledge sometimes leads to overthinking and self-doubt, making her feel disconnected from those who don't share her academic passion. Emily can also get stuck in the cycle of pursuing degrees and validation, losing sight of practical applications.

Public Advocate Archetype

What motivates this Success MNSTR Archetype persona?

Public Advocates are often driven by a deep desire for meaningful change, equity, and social justice. They have a passion for collective action, influencing decision-makers, and establishing a more inclusive society.

What supportive strengths, habits, and behaviors does this Success MNSTR Archetype persona have?

Public Advocates are characterized by their effective communication skills, empathy, and the ability to mobilize and inspire. They're adept at advocating for others, and they listen to diverse voices while collaborating to drive positive societal shifts.

What is the sabotaging dark side of this Success MNSTR Archetype persona?

Public Advocates might neglect their own well-being to help others, experience low self-esteem, or compromise their personal needs for a broader cause. Persistent advocacy can cause burnout, and they might find themselves frequently overwhelmed by the magnitude of their responsibilities.

The Treadmill Trap

Public Advocates can fall into a never-ending cycle of constantly striving to bring about change while still feeling that they need to do more. This relentless pursuit can become overwhelming and feed into the sensation that their efforts are never quite sufficient.

Who fits this Archetype?

Meet Sarah, a nonprofit director who is deeply committed to advocating for social justice and positive change. Her empathetic nature and powerful communication skills enable her to mobilize communities and influence decision-makers. However, Sarah often sacrifices her own well-being for the cause, neglecting self-care as she fights for others. The weight of her responsibilities can feel overwhelming, as she constantly pushes herself to do more, struggling to recognize her progress and the meaningful changes she's already made.

Global Nomad Archetype

What motivates this Success MNSTR Archetype persona?

Global Nomads are driven by their passion for exploration, the freedom to travel when and how they choose, and experiencing other cultures. They are motivated by the prestige of being a global citizen, and seek to share their adventures with others.

What supportive strengths, habits, and behaviors does this Success MNSTR Archetype persona have?

Global Nomads are adaptable solutionists and carry a sense of adventure. Their strengths include thriving in unfamiliar environments and embracing new cultures. They habitually explore and generally value experiences over material possessions.

What is the sabotaging dark side of this Success MNSTR Archetype persona?

The downside of this persona is that feelings of disconnection from those who haven't traveled as much are common, as is finding it challenging to focus in what could be considered more mundane or everyday situations. They can also experience difficulty in forming lasting connections because of their ever-changing surroundings and desire for novelty.

The Treadmill Trap

The incessant urge to seek new experiences can lead to general restlessness and the fear of missing out. This can also cause difficulty when it comes to finding a sense of stability and belonging, thereby perpetuating a cycle of transient adventures without anything to ground the Global Nomad.

Who fits this Archetype?

Meet José, a marketing consultant who thrives on variety and new challenges. He enjoys the freedom of traveling for work and gaining valuable insights from diverse cultures to create unique marketing campaigns. José's adaptability and love for exploration drive his success, but he occasionally struggles with routine tasks. His constant desire for new experiences can lead to restlessness, and he sometimes feels disconnected from colleagues who prefer stability, making it difficult to form long-term professional relationships.

Monarch Archetype

What motivates this Success MNSTR Archetype persona?

Monarchs seek to maintain and even enhance their power, prestige, and family legacy. They seek to establish their authority, make influential decisions, and secure a prominent position for posterity.

What supportive strengths, habits, and behaviors does this Success MNSTR Archetype persona have?

Monarchs display confidence in their leadership qualities and an authoritative demeanor. They're adept at retaining power, ensuring the continuation of their family line, and setting clear guidelines. Their decisiveness, ability to accumulate wealth, and the enjoyment of the benefits of their status are hallmarks of their behavior.

What is the sabotaging dark side of this Success MNSTR Archetype persona?

Monarchs can become obsessed with power and, at times, might place their interests above those of others. Their fixation on control can hinder their innate adaptability and openness toward others' perspectives, leading them to expect or even demand unquestioned compliance.

The Treadmill Trap

While pursuing success and recognition, Monarchs might encounter a sense of emptiness or a lack of genuine purpose. Despite all of their achievements as leaders, they could still feel something is amiss, indicating that success alone isn't providing them with the feeling that they are completely fulfilled.

Who fits this Archetype?

Meet Mohammad, the CEO of a thriving family business, dedicated to maintaining his family's legacy while expanding its influence. His sharp leadership skills and strategic decision-making have elevated his business to new heights. Motivated by the prestige of his position, Mohammad excels at building wealth and ensuring his family's legacy endures. However, his desire for control can sometimes create tension with those who feel unheard. Despite his achievements, Mohammad occasionally feels a lack of true gratification, realizing that power and status alone don't guarantee lasting satisfaction.

Summary

In this chapter, we introduced the nine Success MNSTR Archetypes, each representing unique motivations, strengths, and challenges for high achievers. By identifying your archetype, you gain valuable insights into your behaviors and motivations. Enabling you to better navigate the complexities of success, empowering you to align your goals for greater happiness. After taking the quiz, you'll discover which archetype resonates with you, offering a roadmap to turn challenges into opportunities for growth and lasting success.

3 Key Takeaways:

1. Self-Discovery: Identifying your Success MNSTR Archetype helps you better understand your strengths, motivations, and potential challenges in your journey toward success.

2. Personal Growth: Each archetype offers insights that allow you to align your goals and overcome obstacles, turning challenges into growth opportunities.

3. Community and Connection: Sharing your archetype with others helps foster a sense of belonging, reminding you that many face similar challenges and triumphs.

So, what is your Success MNSTR Archetype?

I'd love to hear from you—share your results with me on any social media platforms. You might be surprised at how many others are experiencing the same challenges and victories as you!

Tag me with **#SuccessMNSTR**

www.successmnstr.com/resources

CHAPTER 4

Rewiring for Success:
The MNSTR Technique
What We Know Today... Step #2

The path to true success requires more than just ambition—it demands an understanding of how our brains work, how to manage societal pressures, and how to prioritize mental well-being. **Step #1** was identifying your Success MNSTR Archetype, helping you recognize both your strengths and potential obstacles.

Now, Step #2 is about enhancing your mindset, challenging societal expectations, building strong support systems, and setting realistic goals that align with your archetype. The MNSTR Technique empowers you to achieve lasting success while safeguarding your mental health. By learning from setbacks and adjusting your approach, you'll find yourself growing stronger, more resilient, and ready to face any challenge.

In the upcoming chapter, "MNSTR in Action," real-life stories will show how this approach works in practice. But before we dive into that, let's take a closer look at what's happening in the world today and then, break down what each letter of the M.N.S.T.R. Technique represents.

In a study published in the online journal Neuron in 2016, researchers examined how the human brain forms enduring habits and pursues goals. Think about those moments when you perform tasks automatically, like brushing your teeth without consciously thinking about it. That's your brain's way of being efficient.

Automatic habit = Unconsciously brushing teeth

Your brain is being efficient

However, sometimes you need to pause and consider your actions, especially when faced with unexpected changes, much like realizing you're going the wrong way and needing to turn around.

Deliberate action = Consciously making a U-turn

Unexpected changes make your brain work harder

Yet, for some individuals, transitioning between these two decision-making modes can pose challenges, potentially leading to conditions such as OCD or addiction. While scientists are still unraveling the brain's mechanisms in this regard, intriguing findings have emerged.

Different parts are responsible for different types of decisions

Conscious thinking

Relying on habits

WATCH OUT!
Your brain can get stuck in habit mode!

Researchers have found that the orbitofrontal cortex (OFC), part of the brain's prefrontal cortex, plays a key role in how we make decisions and form habits.

When the OFC is less active, people rely more on their habits. When it's more active, they are likely to think through their choices more carefully.

For example, when your OFC is highly active, you might take time to carefully decide what to eat for dinner instead of automatically grabbing fast food out of habit. On the flip side, you might react in anger out of habit and later realize it wasn't necessary. Therefore, sometimes, the brain gets stuck in habit mode, even when pausing to think things through would lead to better choices.

Dr. Wendy Wood, from the University of Southern California, found that 43% of everyday actions are done out of habit while people are thinking about other things. Location plays a key role—behaviors repeated in the same place become stronger habits over time.

43% of everyday actions are done out of habit

While people are thinking about other things

The exciting part is that new habits can form by adding small actions to existing routines. In one study, participants integrated a "fabric refresher" into their laundry habits by doing a quick sniff test before deciding to re-wear or wash clothes.

By adding a new action to an existing habit, it becomes easier to remember and maintain. Similarly, habits can be broken or reshaped by changing the triggers behind them. For instance, altering a routine (like taking a different route to work) can disrupt ingrained behaviors, such as buying a daily iced coffee. Understanding these processes helps high achievers make smarter choices, leading to more effective habits.

Changing one's attitude doesn't change one's behavior!

Strong habit-identity helps people maintain
behaviors over time

It's not about changing your attitude—consistent behavior patterns are what drive success, as habits often become tied to personal values and identity. When aligned with these, habits help reinforce a sense of self, making them easier to sustain over time.

The Paradox of Success

Navigating success today reveals a surprising paradox. Society often shows success as effortless, hiding the real struggles behind it. Despite big achievements, many people, including myself, experience "success depression" or "post-success blues" when moving between major goals. If not addressed, this can harm careers and cause organizations to lose valuable talent.

Post-success blues

A 2015 Deloitte study highlighted that 77% of people suffer from career-related burnout, exacerbated by modern hustle culture's demands for prolonged work hours. Similarly, a 2022 report from the World Health Organization (WHO) noted that 15% of working-age adults had a mental disorder in 2019, with 42% quitting their jobs due to exhaustion.

IMPACTING THE WORKFORCE

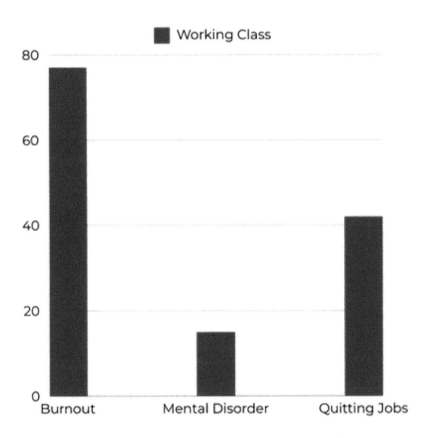

This culture not only fuels emotional and mental strain but also significantly impacts productivity, with depression and anxiety erasing nearly twelve billion work days annually, amounting to a global loss of $1 trillion.

Depression and anxiety cause a global loss
of $1 trillion annually

Erasing nearly twelve billion workdays

In 2019, one in every eight people worldwide was living with a mental disorder, according to the World Health Organization (WHO). The prevalence of anxiety and depression surged by 26% and 28%, respectively, due to the COVID-19 pandemic. Despite the availability of effective treatments, access remains limited, and stigma and discrimination exacerbate the challenges faced by those suffering.

Key WHO Statistics:

Excessive worry and fear

301 million people affected by an anxiety disorder

Anxiety Disorders: In 2019, 301 million people were affected, including significant pediatric cases. These disorders are marked by excessive worry and fear, substantially impairing daily functions.

Persistent sadness and no interest in activities

280 million people affected by depression

Depression: Affecting 280 million people every year, depression involves persistent sadness and a lack of interest in activities, severely impacting life's quality and increasing suicide risks.

While many of us might be unknowingly aware of it, the famous rapper The Notorious B.I.G. once sang, "Mo money, Mo problems." Whether he knew it or not at the time, he was 100% right. For example, Harvard Professor Arthur Brooks found that even high-achieving people having more money didn't make them happier.

"When people see themselves as little more than their attractive bodies, jobs, or bank accounts, it brings great suffering… You become a heartless taskmaster to yourself, seeing yourself as nothing more than Homo economicus."
- Arthur Brooks

A 2016 Marist Institute survey indicated an annual income of $50,000 was identified as a happiness benchmark. While this data predates recent economic shifts such as those caused by COVID-19 and interest rate increases, the underlying principle remains relevant: income disparities have significant psychological impacts on well-being.

The pursuit of highly ambitious goals can often lead to disappointment, highlighting the importance of understanding goal-setting psychology. Janet Polivy and C. Peter Herman's 2002 article in American Psychologist sheds light on potential mental pitfalls, such as the "false hope syndrome."

The "false hope syndrome" is when people set unrealistic goals, like trying to change a habit overnight. They underestimate the effort needed, overestimate the benefits, and expect quick results. When they fail, they don't reassess their goals but instead make another doomed attempt with misplaced confidence. For example, someone might start investing after years of saving, expecting quick returns, but lose interest when the market fluctuates and results are slower than expected.

False Hope

Understanding this success paradox is crucial for high achievers to maintain performance, mental health, and overall well-being. The MNSTR Technique adjusts expectations, strategizes efforts realistically, breaks the cycle of false hope, and fosters true progress.

The Need for a New Technique

Traditional success models often overlook the emotional complexities high achievers face—burnout, imposter syndrome, and relentless pressure to excel. These challenges can overshadow accomplishments, leaving achievers feeling empty despite outward success. True success isn't just about reaching goals; it's about managing emotions, overcoming self-doubt, and thriving.

Take, for instance, an athlete who wins but is crushed by the pressure to keep winning, leading to exhaustion. The MNSTR Technique addresses these struggles, offering a clear, structured way for achievers to navigate the mental and emotional hurdles along the path to lasting success.

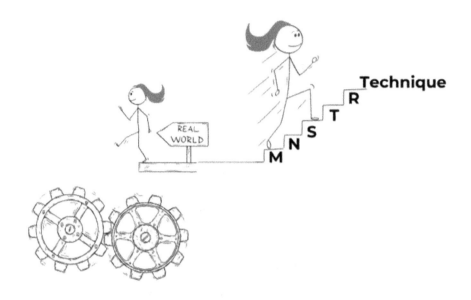

▌Use It When You Need It... Step #2

The MNSTR Technique is your go-to framework when you're feeling overwhelmed, lost, or stuck. Like taking slow, steady breaths to ease a panic attack, this technique helps you regain control by staying present and tuning into your environment, mindset, emotions, and body's reactions.

For example, if you're anxious about a project, the MNSTR Technique helps you identify your stress signals and refocus. Suddenly, what felt daunting becomes manageable, and you're back in control.

Just remember: M. N. S. T. R.

Summary

The MNSTR Technique is a practical tool for high achievers to navigate mental, emotional, and societal challenges. It emphasizes how understanding brain functions, like the orbitofrontal cortex's role in decision-making, can help manage habits and overcome pressure. The technique provides a step-by-step approach to overcoming anxiety, external pressures, burnout, and stress, helping achievers stay on track while prioritizing mental health. Key societal and psychological insights are discussed, such as habit formation, "false hope syndrome," and the paradox of success.

3 Key Takeaways:

1. **Reshape Habit Patterns:** Use insights about the brain's decision-making (OFC) to consciously recognize and break automatic behaviors, creating new, intentional habits.

2. **Manage Success Pitfalls:** Monitor burnout, imposter syndrome, and false hope by adjusting goals to stay emotionally resilient.

3. **Apply the MNSTR Technique for Daily Stress Management:** Use the technique in real-time to manage stressful situations, bringing attention to your physical reactions and mental focus for clearer outcomes by focusing on one letter at a time.

CHAPTER 5

M Stands for Mindset
Defining Mindset

At its core, mindset shapes how we perceive challenges, setbacks, and successes. Your Success MNSTR Archetype highlights these aspects, acting as the mental lens that drives our beliefs and behaviors, ultimately dictating our daily outcomes. Understanding and harnessing this foundational aspect sets the stage for achieving lasting success with the MNSTR Technique.

Growth-oriented Thinking

Based on Dr. Carol Dweck's work at Stanford University, mindsets can be categorized as fixed or growth mindsets. A fixed mindset believes abilities are unchangeable, while a growth mindset believes abilities can improve with effort and persistence. For high achievers, adopting a growth mindset can lead to breakthroughs instead of stagnation.

For example, consider Thomas Edison. Despite failing a thousand times before successfully inventing the light bulb, his growth mindset saw each failure as a learning opportunity, ultimately leading to his breakthrough. This aligns with the Scientist Archetype, where failure is seen as a fast track to answers and discovery.

Benefits of a Growth Mindset

High achievers with a growth mindset have many advantages. They are resilient in setbacks, adaptable in changing environments, and eager to learn and improve. They see failure as part of the learning process and view mistakes as growth opportunities. They strengthen their "failure muscle" with each setback, like reps in a gym. The Athlete Archetype exemplifies this by detecting and correcting themselves during play.

Throughout history, people have turned major setbacks into comebacks. Athletes rebound from defeat, parents find better jobs, and business moguls build empires from failures—all driven by their flexible mindsets.

Ten Strategies for Cultivating a Growth Mindset

GROWTH MINDSET

Intentional   SHIFT YOUR PERSPECTIVE
CONSCIOUSLY CHOOSE YOUR PEERS
Inspirational Media
Physical Environment
POWER NAPS
Gratitude and Appreciation
Cultivating a Beginner's Mindset
HOBBIES
Embrace Failure as Feedback
Self-awareness through Reflection

1. Focus on Increasing Self-awareness through Reflection

The first step to a growth mindset is recognizing where you stand. Through introspection, identify your limiting beliefs by asking,

"How do I feel now?"

"When did I first feel this way?"

"Who influenced this feeling?"

"Is it true?"

2. Cultivate a beginner's mindset

Approach each day with curiosity and openness, maintaining a beginner's mindset to see things from fresh perspectives and learn from every experience. Cultivate continuous learning through workshops, online courses, seminars, or with people who align with your goals. Being a perpetual student keeps the brain agile and receptive to new ideas and skills, and creates enriching neural pathways.

3. Embrace failure as feedback

Regularly step out of your comfort zone by starting new projects, learning new skills, or facing your fears. View challenges as opportunities for growth. See failure as constructive feedback. Embrace growth and exploration to avoid future regrets. Remember, "If your goal doesn't scare you, it's not big enough." This mindset ensures feedback guides you correctly.

4. Consciously Choose Your Peers

It's often said that we become like the people we spend the most time with. Surrounding yourself with individuals committed to personal growth can profoundly influence your own development. These peers act as role models, offering accountability, encouragement, and valuable feedback. Seek out communities or groups aligned with your ambitions to support you on your path to achieving your goals.

Successful peers can also expand your horizons, demonstrating that greater achievements are within reach. For instance, when Roger Bannister broke the four-minute mile record, it inspired countless others to strive for similar feats because they saw it was possible.

5. Shift Your Perspective

Challenges aren't roadblocks; they're opportunities. Shifting your perception of obstacles is crucial. Train your mind to see challenges as chances for growth rather than barriers. Instead of viewing difficulties negatively, focus on finding solutions. High achievers work smart, not just hard. Ask yourself, "What can I learn from this?" and "What is the solution I seek?" rather than dwelling on "the challenge." Approach situations with openness and consider multiple perspectives. This mindset shift can significantly improve your problem-solving approach.

6. Practice gratitude and appreciation

Cultivate a gratitude mindset by reflecting daily on life's blessings and lessons. The ideal time is right before you go to sleep, like a nightly prayer. Appreciate even small positives, like sunshine, a raindrop or a hug. This practice fosters a positive outlook and resilience, helping you handle challenges with grace. When feeling down, ask yourself, "What's one thing I am grateful for?" This simple act builds inner strength and lifts your spirits, even during tough times. For example, if you're having a bad day at work, take a moment to appreciate a kind colleague, enjoy a peaceful lunch break, or blast your favorite song to lift your mood.

7. Curate Inspirational Media

In the digital age, we're flooded with information. Choose to consume positive content to foster a growth mindset. Follow motivational speakers on social media, listen to educational podcasts, and read books that challenge you, like this one. Unfollow anyone who spreads negativity. Worrying about things beyond your control burdens you and disrupts your ability to manage your life. Ensure your media consumption supports your personal growth. For example, instead of watching the news first thing in the morning, start your day with a motivational podcast or a chapter from an uplifting book.

8. Be Intentional with Your Physical Environment

Create a focused environment by reducing distractions and boosting productivity. Keep your workspace tidy (whether it's "Einstein" tidy or simply less cluttered—it helps reduce mental chaos), use a color palette that uplifts you, and display motivational quotes or symbols. Add nature elements like plants and natural light to enhance concentration and mood. For example, I feel happier and more relaxed in a well-organized, aesthetically pleasing space. I find that when my surroundings are messy and chaotic, it creates anxiety and prevents me from focusing on my work. If your space doesn't evoke this sense of calm, consider redesigning it to better reflect your sanctuary.

9. Zero-screen time = hobbies

Regularly unplugging from digital devices helps your brain recover from information overload, improving thinking and decision-making. It also gives you a chance to ground yourself—essentially recharging by connecting with nature (preferably outdoors, and without socks for full effect). Engaging in non-work hobbies boosts creativity and prevents fatigue. For example, wearing a non-digital watch instead of using your phone for the time reduces the temptation to check digital devices, allowing for better focus and relaxation.

10. Power Naps

For high achievers, power naps are essential for peak performance, productivity, enhancing alertness, reaction times, high-level functioning and clearing short-term memory. NASA's studies show that 20 to 30-minute naps significantly boost cognitive functions, memory, and creativity. To avoid grogginess, set an alarm—this is my #1 secret before any work call, performance, or even meeting with friends. The ideal time for these naps is between 1:00 PM and 3:00 PM, during the natural post-lunch energy dip.

Summary

In "M Stands for Mindset," the focus is on how mindset influences a high achiever's ability to navigate challenges and success. By cultivating a growth-oriented mindset, individuals can transform failures into opportunities for learning and advancement. The chapter highlights ten key strategies, from embracing failure as feedback to fostering a positive, intentional environment, all aimed at strengthening resilience and fostering success.

3 Key Takeaways:

1. A growth mindset fosters resilience, helping high achievers adapt and learn from challenges.

2. Curating an intentional environment, including peers and surroundings, enhances focus and motivation.

3. Reflection and self-awareness are essential tools for personal growth, ensuring continuous development and improvement.

CHAPTER 6

N Stands for Neurochemical Understanding

The Brain-based Achievement Connection

Every success, setback, motivation, or indifferent feeling we experience is deeply influenced by the chemicals within our brains and bodies. Understanding these neurochemical processes gives us a distinct advantage in pursuing success, especially when connecting it to your Success MNSTR Archetype. While I'm not a doctor, it's crucial to recognize that these hormones are just a small part of the many functions our brains and bodies perform. By becoming aware of their impact on your mood and decision-making through their activity in your bloodstream, managing them becomes more feasible. This awareness empowers you to recognize and respond to what your brain and body are communicating, enabling you to adjust your course as needed.

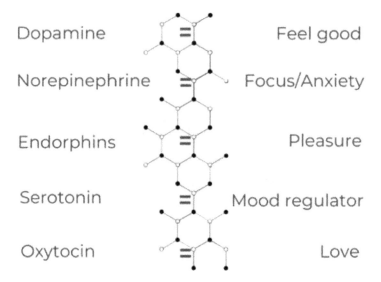

Dopamine — Feel good

Norepinephrine — Focus/Anxiety

Endorphins — Pleasure

Serotonin — Mood regulator

Oxytocin — Love

Dopamine the Superstar Chemical

Dopamine, often labeled as the "feel-good" neurotransmitter, plays a pivotal role in motivation, pleasure, and positive reinforcement. It's made in parts of the brain like the substantia nigra, ventral tegmental area, and hypothalamus, and it responds to the brain's reward system and certain drugs. Issues with dopamine can cause nervous system diseases worsened by stress, poor diet, or stimulants. High achievers are sensitive to dopamine and feel intense motivation from rewards and achievements but risk overdoing them.

For example, after weeks of intense effort, Maria completed her challenging project. As she hit "submit," a surge of dopamine filled her with joy and accomplishment. Sensitive to dopamine, Maria often chased these highs, sometimes pushing herself too hard. That evening, she celebrated with friends, each congratulatory message further boosting her dopamine levels and drive for more.

But while dopamine often steals the limelight, it's important to note that it's just one actor in an ensemble cast. The brain is a marvel of biochemistry; neurotransmitters pull the strings behind the curtains to orchestrate our emotions, actions, and perceptions.

Serotonin

Serotonin, primarily produced in neurons originating from the raphe nuclei in the brainstem, plays a crucial role beyond mood regulation. It influences numerous brain functions and behaviors, with its fibers reaching nearly every brain cell. Serotonin regulates reward processing, sleep, appetite, anger, sexuality, and digestive processes, impacting our overall well-being. It's integral to regulating nearly every human behavior. Maintaining optimal serotonin levels can stabilize emotional fluctuations that may hinder achievement and ambition. Low levels are associated with feelings of low self-esteem and depression, whereas balanced levels foster happiness and confidence.

For instance, before coming to the park, Emma felt depressed and isolated. Hoping to lift her spirits, she decided to take a sunset walk. Sitting on a bench with the warm sun on her face, she watched children play and birds sing. The simple beauty of the moment filled her with peace and a serotonin boost, slowly lifting her out of her gloom and reminding her of life's simple pleasures.

Endorphins

Endorphins are natural chemicals released by your body in response to pain, stress, and pleasurable activities like exercise, massage, eating, and sex. Produced in the pituitary gland and hypothalamus, they act as neurotransmitters that bind to opioid receptors in the brain's reward centers enhancing mood, alleviating discomfort and enabling perseverance through challenges. Physical activity triggers endorphins, leading to a "runner's high" after intense exercise.

For example, after completing her first 10K run, Sarah felt a wave of euphoria. The morning had started with doubts and fatigue, but as she crossed the finish line, endorphins surged through her body. The pain and exhaustion melted away, replaced by a sense of triumph and joy, making all her hard work worthwhile.

Norepinephrine (or Noradrenaline)

Norepinephrine acts as both a neurotransmitter and a hormone, produced in the brainstem and adrenal glands. It plays a crucial role in the "fight-or-flight" response, enhancing alertness and reaction times. However, chronic stress and high levels of norepinephrine can lead to anxiety, hypervigilance, and burnout.

For example, James was constantly overworked and stressed. He dreaded his presentation all week. As he stood in front of the packed conference room, his heart raced and his palms sweated. The surge of norepinephrine sharpened his focus, helping him deliver his presentation with clarity and confidence. By the end, he felt exhilarated, knowing he had conquered his fears. However, the anxiety of the next project made him feel perpetually on alert.

Oxytocin

Oxytocin, often called the "love hormone," is produced in the hypothalamus, a small region at the base of the brain, and released into the bloodstream by the pituitary gland. It regulates social bonding, emotional connections, and aspects of reproductive behavior.

For example, imagine Michelle, who's been feeling isolated and stressed after a tough week. When she meets her close friend for coffee, their deep conversation and laughter trigger a rise in oxytocin. This boost makes Michelle feel more connected and reassured, easing her stress. At the same time, when Michelle's infant is breastfeeding, her oxytocin levels rise again, strengthening her bond with her baby and making the experience feel even more meaningful. Similarly, when Tom spends a weekend playing and reading with his young son, his oxytocin levels increase, deepening their father-son connection and bringing them closer together.

Neurochemical Imbalance and Its Impact

Everything is interconnected

Keep in mind that neurotransmitters don't work in isolation. For example, periods of high dopamine activity, responsible for feelings of elation and motivation, are often followed by a drop, leading to dissatisfaction or emptiness. This dopamine drop can also lower serotonin, the neurotransmitter that regulates mood and anxiety, further contributing to unease. Meanwhile, norepinephrine may surge during stress, increasing alertness but also heightening anxiety. Fluctuations in oxytocin, the hormone tied to bonding and emotional connection, can leave you feeling disconnected or distant after moments of strong social bonding, which temporarily boost oxytocin levels. However, someone who is physically active may regulate these fluctuations more easily, as exercise naturally boosts neurotransmitter activity. Ultimately, highs and lows can occur throughout your day, and feeling good in one moment doesn't guarantee feeling the same way the next.

An example of this is when I prepared for my TEDx Talk. The excitement, preparation, and anticipation initially boosted my dopamine, norepinephrine, and serotonin levels, driving my enthusiasm and focus. However, the intensity of practicing on the TED stage triggered a complex reaction among these neurotransmitters.

After finishing my practice speech and receiving 15 minutes of feedback and coaching, I packed up my things and started walking to my car. As soon as I began driving, I was overwhelmed by a rush that felt like a mini overdose.

Within minutes, I experienced a severe serotonin "letdown." I was missing oxytocin due to the lack of emotional support, and my endorphins, the body's natural painkillers, were depleted from the intense stress and buildup leading up to this day. I began shaking, my hands felt clammy, I had tunnel vision, and I started dry heaving. On the highway, unable to pull over, I talked to myself, desperately trying to make it home safely. Once I got home, I struggled to get inside and collapsed in the bathroom, with my head over the toilet, feeling extremely hot and weak. I could barely move or talk, and my veins seemed to pulse in my head. Finally, I made it to my bed, fully clothed, hoping to pass out. Instead, my body jolted every few minutes, making it one of the worst "let down" feelings I've ever experienced.

Fortunately, by day two of my TEDx practice, I was better prepared, and my body's response to these neurotransmitters was more manageable because I knew what to expect and how to manage it better.

Five Ways to Leverage Neurochemical Knowledge for Sustainable Success

1. Harness Dopamine over Burnout

The path to success doesn't have to be overshadowed by burnout. It's important to note that achieving a so-called "perfect" balance can also lead to burnout. Often, balance is achieved through a cycle of imbalance and adjustment. Basically, balance doesn't exist continually!

Make the best decisions in each moment and keep moving forward. Taking breaks is crucial, as stillness and meditation boost dopamine. It's okay to postpone tasks and prioritize pleasure. Adapt your decisions as circumstances change. Embrace your humanity and the freedom of choice it brings. You don't always have to wait to hit the submit button!

To boost dopamine levels naturally, consider sunlight exposure, exercise, and eating foods rich in healthy proteins, avocados, sesame seeds, probiotics, bananas, etc. Remember, dopamine is just one of the four primary feel-good hormones.

Harness Dopamine over Burnout

Prioritize pleasure

Exercise

Healthy proteins

Take breaks

Make the best choice in the moment

Balance doesn't exist continually!

Athlete Archetypes thrive on dopamine from victories, staying motivated by setting and achieving small goals. **Influencers** get their dopamine from social validation, maintaining their drive through authentic engagement. **Scientists** gain satisfaction from problem-solving, while **Entrepreneurs** feed off new challenges. **Politicians** seek dopamine through public approval, and **Educated** find it in intellectual milestones. **Public Advocates** feel rewarded by the impact they make, **Global Nomads** from new experiences, and **Monarchs** from leadership achievements. For all, setting clear goals and celebrating wins sustains motivation and prevents exhaustion.

2. Prioritize Serotonin Diet and Exercise

Our daily choices significantly influence our brain's chemical balance, from what we eat to how active we are. Choosing nutrient-rich foods and maintaining regular exercise can profoundly impact brain health. A helpful tip is to avoid foods that come packaged in jars, boxes, or bags, as they often contain ingredients that hinder our health.

Integrating exercise into your daily routine is key, especially for those who don't; take short breaks for stretching or do squats while brushing teeth, set up a treadmill at a standing desk, or do sit-ups while watching TV. This way, exercise becomes seamless with your existing activities, removing the need for dedicated workout sessions. Consistent sleep is crucial too; establish a bedtime routine to regulate serotonin levels and overcome common barriers like perceived effort and time constraints.

Prioritize Serotonin Diet and Exercise

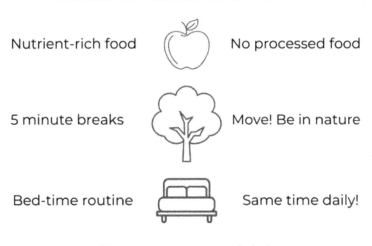

Nutrient-rich food		No processed food
5 minute breaks		Move! Be in nature
Bed-time routine		Same time daily!

Your parents were right!

Serotonin supports emotional stability, mood, and mental clarity across all Archetypes. **Athletes** rely on exercise and diet for peak performance, while **Influencers** enhance it through mindfulness and satisfying activities. **Scientists** and **Entrepreneurs** boost serotonin with a nutrient-rich diet and exercise for focus and stress management. **Politicians, Educated**, and **Monarchs** benefit from healthy lifestyles and positive interactions for effective leadership and decision-making. **Public Advocates** and **Global Nomads** use serotonin to maintain empathy, community engagement, and balance during travel or advocacy work.

3. Activate Endorphins for Resilience

Boost your mood and resilience by integrating various activities into your daily routine. Connect with loved ones, engage in creative pursuits, and find opportunities for laughter. Use relaxation techniques like deep breathing or listening to soothing music to foster calmness. Take short breaks throughout the day to reflect on your feelings, noting what's working and what needs adjustment. For example, you could start your morning with a brief yoga session, enjoy a walk and chat with a friend during lunch, and end your day by sketching or painting. By diversifying your sources of joy and stress relief, you'll enhance endorphin release and build a solid foundation for facing life's challenges with positivity.

Activate Endorphins for Resilience

Endorphins boost performance and recovery for **Athlete Archetypes** by reducing pain and increasing pleasure during intense workouts. **Influencers** and **Entrepreneurs** benefit from enhanced mood and stress relief, maintaining energy and positivity through enjoyable activities. **Scientists** use endorphins to relieve stress and improve focus, while **Politicians** rely on them for composure in public roles. **Educated**, **Public Advocates**, and **Global Nomads** leverage endorphins for resilience, mood stability, and stress management, while **Monarchs** use them to maintain balanced leadership and decision-making through regular exercise and leisure activities.

4. Boost Norepinephrine for Focus and Drive

Alongside dietary choices, staying hydrated and engaging in challenging activities like team sports, public speaking, or tackling difficult tasks at work can boost norepinephrine. Novel and stimulating environments, such as traveling to new places or engaging in adventurous activities, also trigger norepinephrine release. Embracing these experiences leads to increased alertness, focus, and cognitive flexibility, which contribute to sustainable success.

Boost Norepinephrine for Focus and Drive

Tackle difficult tasks

Get competitive

Seek challenges

Travel

Adventurous activities

Norepinephrine enhances focus, alertness, and performance across all Archetypes. **Athletes** boost it through intense training, while **Influencers** and **Entrepreneurs** rely on high-energy activities and new challenges. **Scientists** and **Educated** enhance concentration and cognitive performance with mental exercises, and **Politicians** benefit from it during debates and strategic planning. **Public Advocates** gain motivation from dynamic community events, while **Global Nomads** fuel excitement through exploration. **Monarchs** optimize norepinephrine through challenging leadership roles and strategic initiatives.

5. Embrace Oxytocin for Connection and Support

In addition to nurturing close relationships and fostering trust, simple actions like spending quality time with loved ones, offering or receiving a comforting touch, or participating in supportive group activities can boost oxytocin levels. Engaging in these bonding experiences—whether it's having a heartfelt conversation, sharing a meal, or helping someone in need—can enhance your sense of connection and emotional well-being. This increased oxytocin helps you feel more supported and grounded, fostering deeper relationships and resilience in the face of challenges.

Embrace Oxytocin for Connection and Support

Group activities

Comforting touch

Quality time

Help someone

Relationship building

Oxytocin strengthens connections across all Archetypes. **Athletes** build teamwork and motivation through strong bonds with teammates, while **Influencers** foster genuine connections by sharing real experiences with their audience. **Scientists** collaborate better in group projects, and **Entrepreneurs** build trust within their teams and networks. **Politicians** create public rapport by engaging with communities, and **Educated** benefit from mentor-mentee relationships. **Public Advocates** deepen community ties, **Global Nomads** form connections despite frequent travel, and **Monarchs** ensure loyalty and legacy through meaningful traditions and caring leadership.

Summary

In "N Stands for Neurochemical Understanding," the focus is on how neurotransmitters like dopamine, serotonin, endorphins, norepinephrine, and oxytocin influence success, mood, and resilience. These brain chemicals play a pivotal role in how we pursue goals, handle stress, and maintain emotional balance. By learning to manage these chemicals through diet, exercise, and awareness, high achievers can avoid burnout, enhance their motivation, and achieve sustainable success by keeping their minds and bodies in harmony.

3 Key Takeaways:

1. Dopamine fuels motivation; serotonin balances mood.

2. Endorphins aid resilience; norepinephrine sharpens focus.

3. Mastering brain chemistry leads to long-lasting success.

CHAPTER 7

S Stands for Satisfaction (Intrinsic vs. Extrinsic)

Defining Satisfaction for High Achievers

Satisfaction lies in both the joy of the journey and the accolades at the destination. As we dive deeper into the subject, the distinctions between intrinsic and extrinsic motivations become more apparent, and each plays a pivotal role in achievement.

Why Both Intrinsic and Extrinsic Sources of Motivation Matter

Intrinsic Motivation

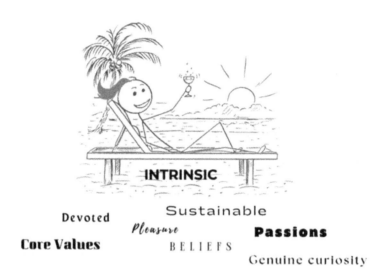

INTRINSIC

Devoted   Sustainable

Pleasure   Passions

Core Values   BELIEFS

Genuine curiosity

The Nature of Intrinsic Motivation

Intrinsic motivation is rooted deeply within an individual's psyche. It is an internal compass, guiding actions based on innate desires, self-driven inspiration, and passion.

Since it does not depend on the presence of tangible rewards, intrinsic motivation remains unaffected by the absence or removal of material or external validation.

The Origins and Benefits of Intrinsic Motivation

For pleasure not awards

Intrinsic motivation comes from a person's core values and beliefs. When an action aligns with these principles, the motivation to act increases. It mainly involves engaging in a task for the pure enjoyment of it, not for external rewards. This type of motivation keeps people engaged and devoted to tasks longer, helping them master skills or subjects. When faced with challenges, those driven by intrinsic motivation are more likely to persevere because their passion, not external rewards, drives them. This brings deep satisfaction, as joy comes from the activity itself.

For example, someone who loves painting doesn't do it for awards or recognition but because they find joy and gratification in the process. Similarly, you might play a sport because you enjoy it, not for a trophy, or spend time with someone you care about because you enjoy their company, not to boost your social status. Or, learning Spanish out of curiosity instead of job necessity shows prioritizing genuine interest over external pressures.

Intrinsic motivation drives each Success MNSTR Archetype differently. **Athletes** seek personal growth through improving their performance, while **Influencers** thrive on genuine engagement and self-development. **Scientists** are fueled by curiosity and discovery, and **Entrepreneurs** by innovation and creating new ventures. **Politicians** are driven by making a meaningful impact, and **Educated** by the love of learning. **Public Advocates** pursue positive social change, **Global Nomads** find fulfillment in exploration, and **Monarchs** are motivated by building a legacy through effective leadership. Each archetype seeks personal satisfaction aligned with their unique goals.

Nurturing Intrinsic Motivation

Regular self-reflection helps clarify personal motivations, guiding people toward their true passions. Staying curious opens the door to discovering new interests, keeping intrinsic motivation strong. While external rewards can motivate us, relying too much on them can overshadow our internal drive. Balancing external recognition with self-motivated goals keeps our inner motivation strong.

"I was worth about over $1 million when I was twenty-three, and over $10 million when I was twenty-four, and over $100 million when I was twenty-five, and it wasn't that important. I never did it for the money."
- Steve Jobs, 1996 PBS documentary
Triumph of the Nerds

Intrinsic motivation provides a fulfilling path to personal growth and achievement. By recognizing and nurturing this motivation, one can find lasting satisfaction in many areas of life.

Extrinsic Motivation

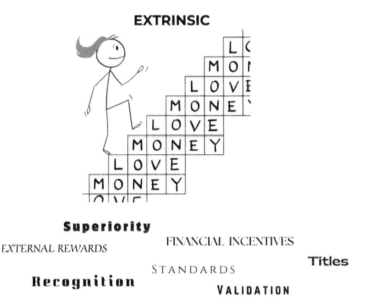

Understanding Extrinsic Motivation

Unlike intrinsic motivation, extrinsic motivation is fueled by external rewards and recognition from our peers. It's the carrot that's dangled in front of someone to encourage a specific behavior or to achieve a particular outcome. This kind of motivation often manifests in material forms.

The Sources and Benefits of Extrinsic Motivation

For money and awards

Extrinsic motivation often comes from financial incentives like salaries, bonuses, and commissions, driving many in their professional pursuits. It also includes social recognition, such as awards, titles, and accolades from professional, academic, or community spaces. This acknowledgment from peers and superiors can be a powerful motivator. Even small-scale validation, like performance reviews, grades, and likes, can push individuals to meet specific standards.

Tangible rewards come with clear criteria for achieving them, offering concrete goals and providing direction and purpose. These rewards serve as proof of one's competency and assurance that their skills and efforts are valued and recognized by others. While intrinsic rewards might take time to appear, extrinsic rewards and recognition provide immediate positive reinforcement, especially useful for short-term behavior changes or when quick results are needed.

For example, a salesperson might strive to exceed their targets to earn a bonus. A student may work hard to get good grades and earn a scholarship. An employee might put in extra effort to receive a promotion or an award at work.

Extrinsic motivation for each archetype focuses on external rewards. **Athletes** chase titles and recognition, while **Influencers** seek likes and followers. **Scientists** are driven by peer approval and publishing success, and **Entrepreneurs** by financial rewards and market recognition. **Politicians** seek public approval and endorsements, while **Educated** aim for degrees and certifications. **Public Advocates** are motivated by media coverage and public support, **Global Nomads** by travel experiences and cultural recognition, and **Monarchs** by the preservation of status, legacy, and power.

The Interplay Between the Two

Can intrinsic and extrinsic motivations coexist harmoniously? Is one better, or does each provide something unique on your path to success?

Complementary Forces

Just as the ancient yin-yang symbol represents two halves forming a whole, intrinsic and extrinsic motivations work together to create a solid foundation for sustainable success. Much like your Success MNSTR!

Intrinsic motivation, driven by personal values and passions, acts as a compass steering individuals based on genuine interest. Extrinsic motivation, offering external rewards and benchmarks, guides them on their journey.

Motivation can shift throughout life, with one form sometimes outweighing the other. For example, a student may study out of genuine interest (intrinsic) while also aiming for top grades (extrinsic). Similarly, a professional might start a career for the salary and promotions but later find satisfaction in mentoring others or mastering their field. However, overemphasizing external rewards can undermine intrinsic motivation, causing individuals to lose touch with their inner drive and values, potentially diminishing their original passion and interest. Balancing both types of motivation is crucial for maintaining sustainable success and personal growth.

Cultivating Intrinsic Motivation in a World of Extrinsic Rewards

In the modern world, where external markers of success dominate the spotlight, maintaining an intense passion for intrinsic values can be a challenge, but it is also a necessity. Society parades tangible rewards in front of us on a constant loop, but it's vital to recognize that true motivation most often comes from within. By reflecting on our goals and setting personal milestones, we can nurture our genuine desires, embrace lifelong learning, and find inspiration in those who prioritize their passions over immediate rewards. Ultimately, redefining success to value personal satisfaction over societal validation is key to a fulfilling journey.

The Role of Societal Conditioning

From birth, societal norms and expectations shape our values, aspirations, and views on success. These cultural templates, passed down through generations, often influence choices like pursuing prestigious careers or achieving traditional milestones like marriage and homeownership by a certain age. However, it's important to understand that these norms aren't universal and may not align with everyone's true desires. Finding the courage to defy these expectations is essential.

By recognizing these external influences, we can make more authentic decisions. The real challenge is staying true to our passions and forging our unique paths despite societal pressures.

Both intrinsic and extrinsic motivations are essential for achieving our goals. They work together, and thinking you need only one can hinder your progress. Balancing these motivations is key to finding genuine satisfaction. By regularly reflecting on and refining your motivations, you can create a life full of passion and accomplishment.

Summary

In "S Stands for Satisfaction (Intrinsic vs. Extrinsic)," the focus is on the dual nature of satisfaction for high achievers, examining both intrinsic and extrinsic motivation. Intrinsic motivation stems from personal values and joy in the process, while extrinsic motivation is driven by external rewards and recognition. The chapter emphasizes how a balance of both types is crucial for sustainable success. It also addresses societal pressures and how to stay true to personal passions amidst external expectations.

3 Key Takeaways:

1. **Intrinsic Rewards Last**: Personal growth and fulfillment sustain motivation in the long term.

2. **Extrinsic Recognition Motivates**: Tangible rewards like awards and social recognition are useful for achieving short-term goals.

3. **Cultivate Inner Drive**: To maintain sustainable success, regularly reflect on personal motivations and values, balancing them with external incentives.

CHAPTER 8

T Stands for Treadmill Management
Understanding the Hedonic Treadmill

Imagine running on a treadmill—you move fast but stay in the same place. Now, think of this treadmill as symbolizing your pursuit of happiness. This concept is known as the hedonic treadmill, a psychological idea where we tend to return to a stable level of happiness regardless of positive or negative events.

For instance, when you acquire something new, it initially brings joy, but over time, that excitement fades, prompting a search for the next new thing to regain that feeling. This hedonic treadmill shows that as we accumulate more, our happiness levels adjust, requiring even greater accomplishments to feel fulfilled again. It's like an addiction where increasing doses are needed to replicate the initial euphoria. This cycle of short-lived happiness keeps us in a continuous state of striving. In today's world, with abundant opportunities and material symbols of success, it often feels like genuine happiness is always just out of reach.

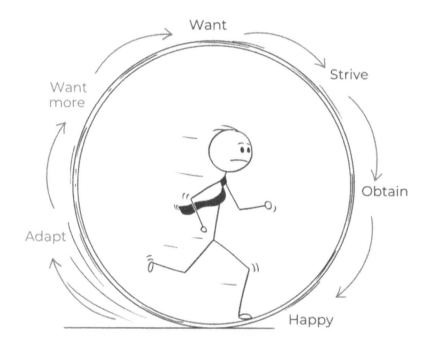

Beyond What Is Tangible

The hedonic treadmill isn't just about material desires; it also involves the relentless chase for recognition and social standing. This quest for validation can be even more consuming, making us wonder if we can ever truly escape the cycle. The key lies in changing how we perceive and value our achievements.

Mastering the hedonic treadmill requires conscious effort. Recognize the endless desire for more and cultivate gratitude for what you already have. By stepping off the treadmill of societal pressures and commercial influences, you can appreciate your current achievements and enjoy the journey toward future goals.

Five Tools to Escape the Hedonic Treadmill

Escape the Treadmill

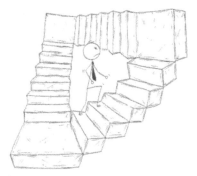

Human Connection · · · · · · · · · · Redefine your success

GOALS FOR YOUR TRUE SELF

BE IN THE NOW · · · · CELEBRATE

1. Embrace the Present Moment

Amid our relentless pursuit of achievements, we often overlook the magic of today, the magic of this very second. Be in the NOW. Take a moment to look up and be grateful for the ability to read this book. Glance around the room and smile at the first object that catches your eye. Then, tell yourself why that object makes you happy. Practicing mindfulness through moments of reflection, body scanning, listening to music, meditation, creative arts or journaling can help us deeply appreciate the present and find grounding in life's journey.

2. Align Goals with Your True Self

In a world where our desires are often shaped by others, it's important to rediscover what truly matters to us. You might still be figuring out who you are, and that's okay—it's a lifelong journey. Embrace not having all the answers as an opportunity to keep learning about yourself. Start by setting small goals: one you can accomplish in a day, another in three days, and another in a week. These should reflect your dreams and the life you want to create for yourself. Additionally, set boundaries to protect your time and energy, ensuring that your efforts align with your personal values and not just societal pressures. When we set goals based on our passions and beliefs, rather than society's expectations, we find lasting happiness instead of just temporary satisfaction from others' approval.

3. Celebrate Simple Joys

Life is brimming with small yet profound moments—a shared smile, a stunning sunset, a child's infectious laughter. We excel at celebrating others, but let's not forget to celebrate ourselves and every single small victory along the way. It's exciting to establish a celebration ritual. How will you mark your next achievement? Perhaps with a dinner outing, your favorite drink, or a rejuvenating long weekend away. This is the joy of celebrating simple pleasures—deciding how we want to commemorate them. By treasuring these everyday experiences, we can counterbalance the relentless pace of the hedonic treadmill.

4. Redefine Success

Instead of seeing success solely as reaching material milestones, consider it a journey filled with valuable experiences. Each day is a page in the chapters of your life. Embrace these experiences. This perspective allows us to appreciate the journey itself, give ourselves grace when things don't work out, and cherish each moment, not just the final outcome. Release expectations about the outcome and its appearance; the end to your story is none of your business anyway. Show up, put in the effort, hold a vision, and then release it; whatever unfolds will unfold. Don't dwell on the question, "How will it happen," just trust that it will!

5. Foster Human Connections

Relationships offer more than companionship; they reflect our values and provide crucial support. Genuine connections guide us through life's challenges, anchoring us in what truly matters and freeing us from life's endless grind. These connections go beyond mere friendships and casual conversations. They allow us to vocalize our thoughts, helping us hear ourselves and solve our own problems. The more human connections we have, the more we realize how little we know, learning from diverse perspectives. However, the right connections make a huge difference. You might have one friend who is a good listener, another who is fun to go out with, and another who is serious. The quality of your relationships, in terms of what they can provide you, is more important than the quantity of friendships.

Then, incorporating appropriate physical touch, like a 10-second hug, boosts immunity, alleviates depression, and reduces fatigue. Extending this to a 20-second hug not only reduces anxiety and stress but also lowers blood pressure and supports heart health. Increasing the frequency of hugs further lowers cortisol levels, enhances healing, reduces cravings, and strengthens immunity. Yes, we've emphasized hugs, but you're grasping the essence—connection is what matters most!

The Happiness Baseline

Everyone has a default level of happiness, known as the "happiness baseline." While life's ups and downs can temporarily affect our mood, we generally return to this baseline. But what if we could adjust this baseline ourselves?

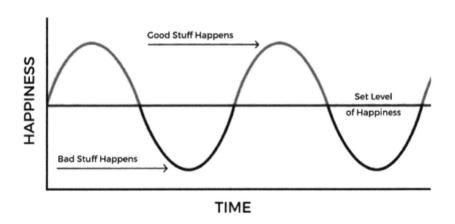

Factors Influencing the Baseline

Genetic Makeup

Just as genes determine physical traits like eye color and height, they also influence our emotional tendencies. Studies by The United Kingdom Biobank suggest that certain genes or gene variants may be linked to our overall happiness levels. However, there's no single "happiness gene"—it's a complex interaction of multiple genes.

Early Life Experiences

The environment we grow up in significantly impacts our emotional well-being. Our attachments to caregivers, school experiences, and early friendships shape our emotional framework. Adverse childhood experiences can affect our emotional health into adulthood, while positive experiences and supportive relationships can strengthen our emotional resilience.

Personality Traits

Some individuals naturally lean towards optimism, while others tend to approach situations with caution or pessimism. These inclinations, shaped by genetics and early life experiences, significantly influence our responses to both challenges and moments of happiness. Personality traits such as extroversion, openness, and conscientiousness are typically associated with higher levels of life satisfaction. Conversely, traits like neuroticism, characterized by anxiety, obsessive behavior, and depression, often correlate with lower levels of happiness.

Boosting your Happiness Set Point

You can positively influence your happiness set point through activities like practicing self-awareness, celebrating small and large life events, improving your diet, continuous learning, meditation, cognitive behavioral therapy and positive social interactions. These activities utilize the brain's ability to change and adapt, known as neuroplasticity.

In short, while many factors determine our baseline happiness, there's always room for improvement. The brain's adaptability gives us hope that we can actively pursue happiness through both external experiences and deliberate internal efforts.

The 4 States of Happiness

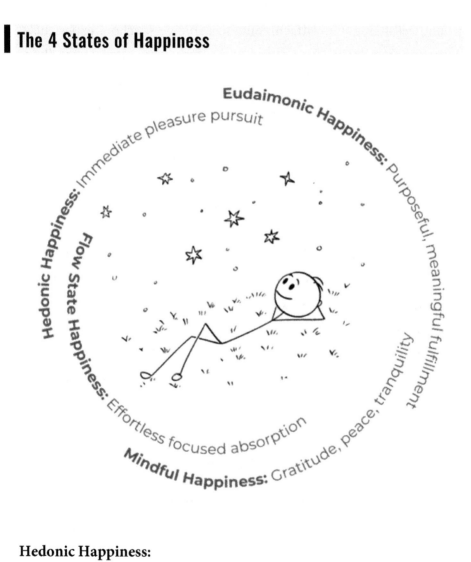

Eudaimonic Happiness: Purposeful, meaningful fulfillment

Hedonic Happiness: Immediate pleasure pursuit

Flow State Happiness: Effortless focused absorption

Mindful Happiness: Gratitude, peace, tranquility

Hedonic Happiness:

Hedonic happiness comes from the pursuit of pleasure and the avoidance of pain. It's the immediate pleasure and excitement that comes from achieving a goal, receiving recognition, or experiencing a positive event. It's the rush of dopamine, the thrill of victory, and the sense of elation that accompanies success. However, this type of happiness can be fleeting and dependent on external validation. It's about doing what feels good.

Hedonic happiness for each archetype focuses on immediate gratification. **Athletes** find joy in winning and personal bests, while **Influencers** thrive on likes and positive feedback. **Scientists** celebrate discoveries and recognition, and **Entrepreneurs** savor business milestones. **Politicians** enjoy election victories and public support, while **Educated** find happiness in earning degrees. **Public Advocates** gain joy from social changes and recognition, **Global Nomads** from new adventures, and **Monarchs** from leadership achievements. Embracing these wins sustains their treadmill happiness.

Eudaimonic Happiness:

Comes from the pursuit of authenticity, meaning, virtue, and growth. This deeper, lasting happiness comes from living a life of purpose. It's the satisfaction of personal growth, connection to something larger than oneself, and the satisfaction of making a positive impact on the world. It's about doing what feels right.

Eudaimonic happiness for each archetype centers on deeper fulfillment through purpose. **Athletes** find it in personal growth and mastery, while **Influencers** align their content with values to create meaningful connections. **Scientists** gain it through contributing to knowledge, and **Entrepreneurs** through building impactful businesses. **Politicians** find purpose in serving the community, and **Educated** through lifelong learning and mentoring. **Public Advocates** focus on justice, **Global Nomads** through cultural immersion, and **Monarchs** by upholding a lasting legacy with meaningful leadership. Each archetype seeks satisfaction through purpose-driven actions.

Flow State Happiness:

Mihaly Csikszentmihalyi discovered that people find genuine satisfaction in a state of consciousness called Flow. This state is characterized by complete absorption in a challenging activity, where time seems to disappear and one feels effortless control. It occurs when your skills perfectly match the task, leading to intense focus, enjoyment, and creativity.

Flow state for each archetype centers around deep focus and immersion. **Athletes** achieve it through challenging goals and disciplined practice, while **Influencers** find it in content creation when focusing on passion projects. **Scientists** reach flow in deep research, and **Entrepreneurs** in innovative tasks. **Politicians** experience it during policy-making and public speaking, while **Educated** find it in focused study. **Public Advocates** enter flow during advocacy work, **Global Nomads** during immersive travel, and **Monarchs** through focused leadership tasks. For all, eliminating distractions and focusing deeply is key to flow.

Mindful Happiness:

It's the ability to appreciate the small joys in life, to find beauty in the ordinary, and to cultivate gratitude for all that we have. This type of happiness is less dependent on external circumstances and more rooted in inner peace and tranquility.

Mindful happiness enhances performance across archetypes by promoting presence and balance. **Athletes** stay focused during training, while **Influencers** manage social media stress by prioritizing genuine interactions. **Scientists** boost concentration by staying calm, and **Entrepreneurs** handle business pressures more effectively. **Politicians** enhance empathy and composure, **Educated** improve learning, and **Public Advocates** maintain resilience. **Global Nomads** deepen their travel experiences by being present, while **Monarchs** strengthen leadership with balanced decisions. Mindfulness helps each archetype stay grounded and perform at their best.

Summary

In "T Stands for Treadmill Management," the focus is on understanding the **hedonic treadmill**—the cycle where high achievers chase temporary satisfaction, constantly seeking more to maintain happiness. The chapter introduces strategies to break this cycle, like practicing mindfulness, setting aligned goals, and celebrating small wins. Additionally, it emphasizes the **happiness baseline**—the level of contentment we return to—and explains how it can be improved through mindset shifts, personal reflection, and intentional action to find lasting self-realization.

3 Key Takeaways:

1. **Recognize the Hedonic Treadmill**: Learn to identify when you're caught in a loop of chasing temporary highs and shift focus.

2. **Elevate Your Happiness Baseline**: Through self-awareness, gratitude, and mindfulness, you can raise your baseline and sustain long-term happiness.

3. **Balance the Four Types of Happiness**: By incorporating hedonic, eudaimonic, flow, and mindful happiness, you achieve more consistent and deeper fulfillment.

CHAPTER 9

R Stands for Restoration of Motivation and Wellness

Balancing Success with Well-Being

High achievers often thrive on the adrenaline rush of motivation. However, motivation and wellness are closely linked; a decline in one often leads to a decline in the other. How do we restore balance when they're out of sync?

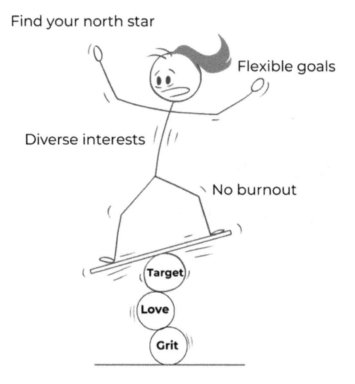

Find your north star

Flexible goals

Diverse interests

No burnout

Target

Love

Grit

Understanding Burnout

Burnout is deep emotional, mental, and physical exhaustion that anyone can experience. It stems from busy lives filled with work, caregiving, and family duties. High achievers are especially prone to this due to the pressure for perfection and constant stress. Exhaustion reduces productivity, creates feelings of hopelessness and resentment, and impacts home, work, and social life. Long-term fatigue can even weaken the immune system. For example, consider how often you get sick or how frequently you postpone simple tasks because you feel overwhelmed. Recognizing early signs is crucial for dealing with and overcoming it.

Some people may not believe in burnout, but it can appear in various ways that harm overall well-being. No matter what you call it, these cycles will happen. It's okay to feel tired, but there comes a point where you must acknowledge when enough is enough and not ignore it any longer. Focusing on personal well-being needs to become your top priority.

Finding Your North Star

In the pursuit of success, it's easy to lose sight of our true motivations. Self-observation is crucial for reconnecting with the passions that initially inspired us. Review whether the life you are living is what you envisioned or if it feels like a crazy mess where you're a rat running on a wheel with no end in sight. For example, are you dedicating time each week to activities aligned with your North Star, or are you caught in a cycle of routine without questioning its purpose?

Flexible Goals

In a constantly changing world, rigid goals can lead to disappointment. Our aspirations should evolve with our personal growth and experiences. What works for one person may not work for another. It's powerful to set goals, stay open to possibilities, and trust that things will unfold as they should. Show up, take action, ask questions, explore options, and let events unfold naturally without rushing.

Regularly reviewing and adapting our goals keeps them relevant and inspiring. It's also important to know when to let go of a goal that no longer serves you. For example, someone might want to become a police officer because of the exciting portrayal on TV, but after enrolling, they find that much of the job is paperwork, which they dislike. This would be a good time to change the goal before it's too late.

Embracing Diverse Interests

Focusing all your energy on one passion can be limiting. Exploring various interests keeps us energized. Having diverse passions ensures long-term enthusiasm and gratification. If you're deeply invested in a passion project, that's great, but what else are you doing? Once you finish that project, you might feel a sense of letdown or feel lost without a goal. This book will help you when that happens, but consider expanding into related areas of your current goal to stay focused while diversifying your interests.

For example, if you're an athlete training for a marathon, you could also explore nutrition, coaching others, or participating in different types of physical activities like yoga or cycling to keep your enthusiasm high and prevent exhaustion.

Guiding Principles for Motivation:

It's interesting how some people wait to feel motivated before taking action, but that approach can be a double-edged sword. If you wait for motivation to strike, you might find yourself waiting indefinitely. High achievers understand the importance of stepping into action even when motivation is lacking. This proactive approach provides a sense of control and direction. As momentum builds and progress is made, motivation naturally follows. Author Victor Vroom shares that motivation depends on two things:

Expectation*: Believing that a specific action will lead to a desired result.*

Value of the Outcome*: How important that result is to the person.*

For example, if you believe that studying hard will result in good grades and you highly value those grades, you will be motivated to study hard. People are motivated when they expect their efforts to lead to successful results, and the more valuable the outcome, the more motivated they will be to achieve it.

Therefore, motivation = belief in success × value of the result.

A more focused way I break it down is by using **Target, Love, Grit:**

1. ***Target:*** *Define your desired outcome to stay focused.*
2. ***Love:*** *Your passion fuels the energy you invest in your efforts.*
3. ***Grit:*** *Psychological endurance helps you overcome obstacles along the way.*

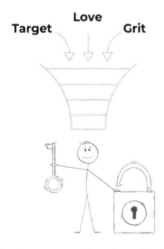

The key to sustained motivation

In short, sustained motivation = goal × amount of love for it × willingness to deal with difficulties.

So you have to ask yourself, have you clearly identified your target, assessed your level of passion for it, and determined if you have the grit to persist? If not, this could be why you are spinning out, losing motivation, starting something but never finishing it, and ultimately not achieving your goals.

Fostering Well-Being for Lasting Peak Performance

Physical well-being

Social harmony

EMOTIONAL & PSYCHOLOGICAL RESILIENCE

Spiritual wellness

Physical Well-being

A healthy body is essential for a resilient mind. High achievers know the importance of nutritious eating, regular exercise, and ample sleep. While these principles are widely recognized, the critical question is: when will you prioritize your health?

Often, people who have reached their professional or financial goals start focusing on their well-being. You may have noticed them sharing insights on red-light therapy, cold plunges, neurofeedback brain training, sleep enhancement devices, and personalized supplements. These folks achieved their 'success milestone' and now it has opened up the space to focus on themselves because traditionally, they went through hell and are now back with an action plan to not go through it again.

You have a choice: wait until you've achieved everything or start prioritizing your health now and make it part of your journey to success.

Emotional and Psychological Resilience:

Navigating high achievement involves confronting significant stressors. To thrive, high achievers actively build emotional resilience through various strategies: engaging in creative activities like art, music, writing, or dance; participating in physical activities such as hiking, rock climbing, or martial arts; and joining support groups or community organizations. These methods help manage intense emotions, foster mental clarity, and sustain well-being by strengthening their resilience muscle. This is further explained in Chapter 6, Neurochemical Understanding, ensuring a strong foundation for continued success.

For example, the different Success MNSTR Archetypes can help guide your approach. An Educated Archetype might find resilience in learning new skills or diving into research, while an Influencer might draw strength from social connections and community support. The Athlete Archetype could benefit from physical challenges and setting personal records, and a Public Advocate might find resilience through activism and helping others. By aligning your strategies with your archetype, you can better manage stress and build emotional strength.

Social and Relational Harmony

Human connections are crucial for support. Friends, family, and mentors provide strength during tough times. However, many high achievers may struggle to find like-minded individuals and often need to be proactive, attending conferences and events to connect with peers who understand their daily challenges. It's important to be patient in finding your tribe; high achievers are a unique group, not easily found. While human connection is vital, being comfortable with solitude is also essential. When you do find kindred spirits, setting boundaries ensures relationships remain supportive rather than draining, balancing personal and professional demands effectively.

Spiritual Wellness

Finding deeper meaning and connecting to a larger purpose can inspire lasting fulfillment. Whether through religion, spirituality, or personal introspection, explore what resonates with you and consider stepping outside your comfort zone. This might involve prayer, meditation, chanting, breath work, or other rituals that foster connection and compassion with your higher-self. Embrace your unique journey, seek guidance, practice regularly, and embrace the unknown. Spiritual wellness encompasses relationships, values, and a meaningful life purpose that provides solace and motivation in the pursuit of your goals.

Summary

In "R Stands for Restoration of Motivation and Wellness," the focus is on balancing high achievement with well-being. The chapter highlights the importance of recognizing and addressing burnout, realigning goals with personal motivations, and fostering a holistic approach to wellness, including physical, emotional, social, and spiritual aspects. By understanding when to take breaks, cultivate diverse interests, and build resilience, high achievers can maintain sustained motivation while ensuring they don't sacrifice their health and happiness for success.

3 Key Takeaways:

1. **Monitor Energy Levels:** Regularly check for signs of burnout and take immediate steps, such as setting boundaries or adjusting your workload, to prevent emotional and physical exhaustion.

2. **Adjust Goals Regularly:** Review and realign your goals frequently to ensure they match your passions, keeping you motivated without feeling trapped by outdated ambitions.

3. **Integrate Wellness Habits:** Establish daily routines that address physical, emotional, and spiritual health, such as exercise, mindfulness, and social connections, to sustain motivation and avoid exhaustion.

CHAPTER 10

The MNSTR Technique in Action

Yes, it's an acronym—utilize it!

Success stories often glorify achievements while overlooking the accompanying struggles. High achievers, despite their outward success, often battle depression in private, pressured to maintain appearances. Let's explore real-life stories of struggle, "aha" moments, and practical use cases on how individuals have overcome their challenges. By sharing these short narratives, my aim is for you to reflect on your own obstacles and apply the MNSTR Technique in real-time. You can focus on each letter in the MNSTR acronym or only a few of them.

This approach helps you quickly spot signs, manage symptoms, and use effective tools to move forward in your goals.

Transforming Struggles into Success Stories with the MNSTR Technique

To truly grasp the irony of feeling deep despair after achieving any kind of success, big or small, you have to experience it yourself. You may not have realized it until now, but with every single check on your to-do list, you get a rush of happiness followed by a feeling of sadness. This effect only intensifies with bigger goals, leading to bigger drops after accomplishment. I've condensed these shared experiences into an easy-to-understand framework about obtaining goals and how to start again afterward.

Many people aren't ready for this fall. It's important to redefine success to include both the highs and lows. By applying the MNSTR Technique to real stories, we can uncover the struggles of the go-getters, self-motivators, the high achievers, highlighting their vulnerabilities and challenges. Recognizing these struggles helps future generations prepare for both their victories and hardships.

MNSTR

IN ACTION

Do any of these short stories sound familiar?

| Story #1: Uncharted Entrepreneur

John's Success MNSTR archetype: **Educated**

The Educated Archetype thrives on knowledge and intellectual growth, excelling in research and critical thinking. However, they can overthink, doubt themselves, and appear elitist. They may also get trapped in endless validation instead of applying their knowledge.

John's entrepreneurial journey began with high hopes. Starting from his garage, he brought an idea to life and saw it take off. However, he soon faced a mountain of debt, a betrayal by his business partner, and declining health due to stress. Confronted with bankruptcy, John's initial optimism turned into tormenting doubts about whether his dreams were worth the struggle or if they had ultimately betrayed him.

MNSTR in Action

M: Mindset

John shifted his mindset from fixed to growth, viewing failures as feedback rather than dead ends. He realized he was strengthening his "failure muscle," making it robust enough to support his journey through the hardships he was experiencing. This change enabled him to perceive challenges as "solutions," and he began to see opportunities, answers, and connections that helped him get back on top. Additionally, he cleared his screen time and curated his environment by removing negative reminders from his social and online life.

N: Neurochemical Understanding

John learned to recognize his neurochemical responses effectively. When he felt a rush of chemicals that made him feel sick, dizzy, or short of breath, he paused and reassured himself, "I recognize this feeling; it's normal, and it will pass." He set small, achievable goals to address his needs, boosting dopamine. He practiced gratitude each time he had an insight and spent time in nature to increase serotonin. John exercised and practiced deep breathing to regulate norepinephrine, and engaged in relaxation activities to stimulate endorphins. This holistic approach helped him stabilize his mood and maintain motivation.

R: Restoration of motivation and wellness

John restored his health through regular exercise, eating healthier, scheduling breaks, taking naps, asking for help from mentors and regularly staying in touch with loved ones. These practices brought him peace and vitality, rejuvenating his spirit and enabling him to face challenges with renewed strength, while maintaining motivation.

Empowered by key pillars of the MNSTR Technique, John transformed his struggling startup into a thriving success story. His steadfast commitment and personal growth not only inspired others but also proved that overcoming adversity and achieving greatness is possible with the right tools and mindset. Evolving from a mere entrepreneur, John became a beacon of hope for those navigating similar challenges.

Story #2: Lily's Masterpieces

Lily's Success MNSTR archetype: **Influencer**

The Influencer craves popularity and validation, thriving on positive feedback and a growing fan base. They excel in self-promotion, networking, and communication. However, they can become too dependent on external approval, struggle with authenticity, and face burnout from constantly chasing likes and followers.

Lily's brushstrokes were more than just pigment on canvas; they were pieces of her soul. As the world fell in love with her art, the weight of her newfound fame began to wear her down. Anxiety-clenched fingers gripped her heart every time she faced a blank canvas, stunting her creativity. Each critique, no matter the negativity or praise it contained, echoed with expectation, sending her spiraling into a dark abyss of self-doubt and despair.

MNSTR in Action

S: Satisfaction. Intrinsic vs. extrinsic

Lily's turmoil stemmed from an unquenched thirst for validation. Through deep introspection, she yearned to rediscover the pure joy of creation without worrying about the world's perception—just like the good old days. This realization allowed her to distinguish her love for art from the fleeting high of applause and accolades.

T: Treadmill Management

Recognizing the dangers of the hedonic cycle—the constant chase for praise and recognition—Lily rooted herself in her core passion by reflecting on why she started in the first place. She acknowledged the cycle of emotional highs and lows and aimed to minimize these fluctuations, making them more manageable, like a resting heartbeat. Lily learned to value her internal compass by curating the media she consumed and choosing her social interactions carefully, focusing on what truly mattered to her.

With renewed vigor and clarity, Lily's art underwent a transformation. Her creations, once influenced by public opinion, now expressed raw emotion and truth. They chronicled her journey of self-discovery, becoming profoundly poignant. These works were not just paintings but narratives of resilience and hope. Despite continued admiration, Lily's true triumph was the harmonious song her soul was singing once again. She didn't let her Success MNSTR overtake her; instead, she used the technique to manage and control it, allowing her authentic voice to shine through in her art once again.

Story #3: The Executive Rediscovering His Purpose

David's Success MNSTR archetype: **Monarch**

The Monarch Archetype seeks power, prestige, and a lasting legacy, driven by authority and decision-making. They are confident leaders who accumulate wealth but can become obsessed with control, limiting their adaptability. Despite their success, they may feel unfulfilled, indicating that power alone isn't enough for true satisfaction.

From afar, David seemed to embody success: commanding a successful company from a glass tower with accolades adorning his office. However, beneath this facade lurked profound disillusionment. Despite his outward achievements, David harbored a deep disdain for the corporate world. His relentless pursuit of making the company money had diverted him from his true passions. The long hours and stifling corporate rules imprisoned him in a life far from his youthful dreams. Now, adrift in uncertainty, David grappled with an identity crisis, unsure of who he had become and what he truly wanted in life.

MNSTR in Action

N: Neurochemical Understanding

David learned to appreciate the neurochemical activities in his brain. He realized his relentless pursuits were driven by dopamine, linked to achievement. However, he had neglected serotonin, which brings well-being, and oxytocin, which fosters love and connection. His high-stress lifestyle had likely increased norepinephrine, causing anxiety. Understanding the importance of endorphins, he incorporated exercise and laughter to trigger their release to balance out his moods.

S: Satisfaction. Intrinsic vs. extrinsic

David's journey of self-discovery revealed the limits of chasing external rewards. Reflecting on his youthful passions, he reconnected with his intrinsic values. He extended this exploration to his workplace, encouraging coworkers to share their own youthful stories. This process reignited his internal passions, shifting his focus from external validation to inner fulfillment. Aligning with his true desires brought David a deeper and more sustainable sense of satisfaction, renewing his sense of purpose and joy.

R: Restoration of motivation and wellness

David dug deep into self-restoration through therapy, addressing insecurities, mending old wounds, and reassembling his identity. This process reignited his motivations for a new target, strengthened his love for friends and family, and fortified his grit.

David's leadership style transformed as well. He became a beacon of holistic success, infusing empathy, purpose, and understanding into his decisions. The boardroom, once dominated by cold statistics, now resonated with stories of dreams, aspirations, and human connections. He even started a passion project to work on as he gradually transitioned from the corporate world.

Story #4: The Athlete's External Pressures

Sara's Success MNSTR archetype: **Athlete**

The Athlete Archetype is driven by a passion for excelling and recognition, always striving to be the best. They exemplify discipline, perseverance, and a strong work ethic. However, they may struggle with self-criticism, an obsession with perfection, and perpetual dissatisfaction, constantly chasing the next win without enjoying their achievements.

For Sara, each gleaming trophy was double-edged. With every victory lap, the relentless glare of the spotlight intensified, and the chains of expectations tightened. Her sporting prowess became intertwined with national pride. The media's prying eyes dissected her every move, on and off the field, and personal betrayals threatened to dull her edge. But the final blow was a devastating loss, sending shockwaves through her psyche. The ensuing mockery seemed inescapable, making her feel like a stranger in the very sport she once dominated with love. Thoughts of forsaking her passion, of abandoning the arena, began to cloud her horizon.

MNSTR in Action

M: Mindset

Sara took a step back to journey within herself. She needed to quiet the surrounding noise to rediscover her inner voice, her true cheerleader. She dove into her old scrapbooks, revisited childhood games, and spent silent moments journaling about her past feelings. After a week, she reread her journal from start to finish and noted down the powerful, positive words she had used to describe herself, her lessons, her wins and her many challenges. She created an "I did it list," a portable reminder she could carry everywhere to reconnect with the hard-won battles she had fought, and to reinforce what her mind focused on. It wasn't just about victories; it was about the spirit, the struggle, the passion, and the dialogue she had with her MNSTR. That became her winning mindset.

S: Satisfaction. Intrinsic vs. extrinsic

Sara's journey took her further from her true goals as she focused solely on winning—for her team, and recognition. But when everyone turned against her abruptly, it was a harsh awakening. All her sacrifices, the toll on her body, seemed worthless without victory. She realized her drive was fueled solely by external validation, not her own satisfaction anymore. Feeling unbalanced, she fought to reclaim her original goals. It wasn't about admiration or money anymore. Now, it was about shining a light on women in sports, the next generation and advocating for a cause she deeply believed in since her early days as a young athlete.

The next chapter of Sara's career was more than sports pages' headlines or gleaming trophies. It was the narrative of a heart refusing to be boxed by external definitions, a spirit flying free. Her games became more than competitions; they were poetic dances of love, passion, and undying commitment to her sport, paving the way for all the little girls who dare to dream.

Story #5: The Struggles of Self-Discovery

Alex's Success MNSTR archetype: **Public Advocate**

The Public Advocate Archetype is driven by a desire for justice and meaningful change. They excel in communication and mobilizing others but may neglect their well-being and experience burnout. Their relentless pursuit of change and helping others can make them feel their efforts are never enough.

At the outset, Alex had numerous personal and professional achievements. However, after a diagnosis, she plunged into an identity crisis, feeling disoriented and disillusioned. To find clarity, she embarked on a self-discovery journey through therapy, confronting issues from her upbringing, particularly with her parents. She invested in learning new skills through books, podcasts, and workshops. Despite her efforts, Alex faced resistance from friends and family who struggled to appreciate her newfound insights and tired of her unsolicited advice and epiphanies.

This isolation deepened her despair; she longed to be understood and acknowledged for the trials and tribulations she faced. She sought recognition from the key individuals who had hurt her, hoping they would accept their role in her emotional state. However, their refusal pushed her to withdraw from both her career and social interactions.

MNSTR in Action

M: Mindset

Alex embraced the power of a beginner's mindset. When confronted with anger or frustration, she paused, took a deep breath, and assessed the situation in the moment. Practicing gratitude, she listed three things she was thankful for and fostered empathy towards herself, guiding change with self-compassion. Reflecting on her worthiness, she shed self-doubt and learned when to step away for emotional balance. By setting healthy boundaries, questioning limiting beliefs, and evaluating her impact, she moved forward with self-reflection and renewed empowerment.

N: Neurochemical Understanding

Armed with newfound knowledge of neurochemistry, Alex learned to recognize how her thoughts and emotions impacted her brain chemistry. When overwhelmed by anger or sadness, she connected with her body, identified where the discomfort resided, and questioned why it was there and whether it was true. She visualized the negative energy leaving through her fingertips and toes, releasing it until the rush subsided.

To boost dopamine levels, Alex engaged in activities that brought her joy, like crafting. Serotonin flowed when she practiced gratitude, spent time in nature, or accomplished small tasks that gave her a sense of satisfaction. For increased norepinephrine, she maintained a regular exercise routine and practiced deep breathing. By understanding these neurochemical surges, Alex embraced them as tools to achieve her desired outcomes.

S: Satisfaction. Intrinsic vs. extrinsic

Alex came to understand that true satisfaction comes from within. She acknowledged that her friends and family might never fully understand her journey but found peace in knowing that their support, when offered, was enough. She released the need to educate everyone about her challenges, recognizing that seeking external validation wouldn't fix the problem. Instead, Alex focused on listening to those around her and finding joy in connecting by understanding them.

R: Restoration of motivation and wellness

Alex prioritized her well-being, replenishing her own cup before tending to others. She stepped away from societal pressures to focus on her own needs and desires. To restore motivation, she identified small new targets, assessed her passion for them, and strengthened her perseverance to navigate the inevitable ups and downs.

Alex, who lost her identity, embarked on a journey of self-improvement fraught with challenges. Armed with the MNSTR Technique, she overcame each obstacle one step at a time. Embracing a growth mindset, she navigated her emotions, practiced gratitude, set boundaries, and challenged limiting beliefs. Understanding neurochemistry, she harnessed the power of dopamine, serotonin, and norepinephrine to fuel her growth and well-being. Recognizing that true satisfaction comes from within, Alex embraced minimalism and let go of seeking external validation. By prioritizing her well-being and restoring her motivation, she emerged victorious, ready to navigate life's peaks and valleys once again.

Story #6: Barely Breathing to Fully Alive (My Story)

Ashley's Success MNSTR archetype: **Entrepreneur**

Entrepreneurs are motivated by financial control, autonomy, and the freedom to create a lifestyle reflecting their values. They are innovative, independent, and proactive, but may struggle with self-doubt and exhaustion from the relentless pursuit of success. This constant chase can lead to neglecting balance, resulting in emotional and physical exhaustion.

After achieving the largest digital launch in my partnership's history—a crowning achievement in a career marked by many losses and triumphs—an unexpected void opened up before me. The thrill of professional success quickly gave way to deep self-doubt, despair, and identity loss. Financial challenges from unexpected money management tainted the victory, leaving a bitter taste. This entire success was intertwined with my partnership, leaving me anxious daily about my ability to support my family if it faltered. I had no other streams of income at the time. Panic attacks, emotional paralysis, and shattered self-esteem overwhelmed me, pushing me to contemplate the unthinkable: ending my own life.

MNSTR in Action

M: Mindset

As a former athlete and coach, I was familiar with the mindset game. I'd been through highs and lows before, but during this period, a darker side of me emerged—angry, desperate, almost possessed. My family couldn't be around me without me exploding over trivial things. I became brutal—a grade-A asshole. There was no positivity unless I was faking it, which I did often. It felt like all the gratitude and optimism I had cultivated over 42 years had vanished.

*Fear and negativity consumed me.
My Success MNSTR was winning.*

Even recognizing myself became difficult. Despite my natural optimism and tendency to view failure as a stepping stone, I struggled deeply.

As I began opening up to a few people about my behavior and poor decisions, they reminded me of my natural strengths. This wasn't my first roller coaster of highs and lows, and I knew it wouldn't be my last. Reflecting on past cycles pushed me to dig deeper into why these patterns persisted.

Regaining a positive mindset became crucial, and I drew strength from my spouse, whose joyful, comedic, empathetic, and confident nature became my rock. I started focusing on small joys and moments of gratitude—sunlight through leaves, flowers at the market, comfort food, and family snuggles. Using the Success MNSTR technique regularly, I reverse-engineer my decisions and goals. I'm careful about social media, choosing what content I consume purposefully. Power naps are essential for maintaining energy. While finding new hobbies is ongoing and negative self-talk still creeps in, I've asked friends to help keep me in check. Staying aware has made self-sabotage easier to manage—because let's face it, I'm awesome!

N: Neurochemical Understanding

I often felt terrible and couldn't pinpoint why—it was like throwing darts at a board, hoping one would hit the reason. Initially, I thought my poor habits around eating and sleeping were to blame.

Given my background as a raw food vegetarian and natural health practitioner, I knew the importance of nutrition, but I soon realized that much of the problem wasn't physical—it was my operating system.

Whenever I thought about the future and its uncertainties, I felt dread—a dark, gaping hole opening up. Then the voices followed, taunting me: "You suck, you're a failure, you'll never do better, you're a fraud." Each one left me breathless, as though an elephant sat on my chest.

As I explored how our brains handle goals, I discovered the brain's reward system—how chemicals like dopamine, serotonin, and endorphins flood our system when we succeed. But once those 'feel-good' chemicals wear off, we often experience an emotional 'let-down.' After my first TEDx practice, I felt this intense surge, followed by a crash, like an overdose of these chemicals.

This taught me how easily we can get caught chasing these "mind drugs," seeking that next high, even when it's fleeting.

Now, I handle successes and setbacks like a seasoned skier once again, carving the slopes without catching an edge. Sure, I still have my moments, screaming like a kid on a rollercoaster, but now I know the ride will end. Control is a beautiful thing!

You don't need a degree to understand this—just pause and recognize the chemicals flooding your body during tough moments and happy moments. Treat your brain like a computer, with emotions and physical responses as outputs. Eventually, those chemicals stop pumping, and you start to feel better. It's a cycle, but at least now, I'm prepared for it.

S: Satisfaction. Intrinsic vs Extrinsic

I always told myself success wasn't just about money, but deep down, I still desired the luxuries. In Mexico, it was easy to be a minimalist with nothing to spend money on. However, back in Canada, consumerism took over. Everything I wanted was just a click away, and I indulged in it all—matching pillows, blankets, decor—whatever was on my vision board.

I spent freely on myself, family, and friends without caring about the cost. But every time I checked my bank balance, anxiety crept in. Thoughts of lottery winners who went broke haunted me. If I couldn't manage small amounts of money, how could I handle more?

Old beliefs surfaced: that I'd never have enough or that being rich was somehow wrong. These cycles led me to make money and then blow it all just to rebuild everything from scratch.

But I couldn't keep burning my life down. I didn't have the energy to keep starting over.

Ashamed and lacking income outside my partnership, I withdrew, distancing myself from loved ones. The praise I received felt hollow, and I downplayed my success, feeling unworthy. The weight of my choices became unbearable, but I realized I wasn't alone. Many high achievers stumble after their greatest successes, but few talk about it.

Those who weathered similar storms turned inward, focusing on personal growth and living a more intrinsic lifestyle. I watched others embrace self-improvement—meditation, cold plunges, red-light therapy, stem cell treatments, journaling, and more. Like them, I was rebuilding myself after success. After getting everything I thought I wanted, I realized I no longer needed or cared for most of it. I craved a simpler life. This realization brought me back to personal growth and inspired the Success MNSTR and MNSTR Technique, tools that now guide me through future successes and their inevitable chaos.

T: Treadmill Management

Starting a new goal is always exciting, but the thrill fades quickly once it's achieved. To fill that void, I aimed for bigger, scarier challenges. My mantra was simple: if a goal doesn't scare you, it's not big enough. Yet, no matter how much I accomplished, true happiness remained elusive. I always craved more, driven by my inner athlete's belief that life is short and full of mountains to climb.

But during this dark phase, even those new goals felt fragile, as if I were walking on eggshells. Each major success brought a fleeting rush, but the excitement wore off quickly, leaving me back at square one, feeling like my life had been burned down again.

I eventually had a profound realization: no matter how much we achieve, we all fall into this hedonic treadmill—always running but never quite satisfied. High achievers especially tend to diminish their past accomplishments, always striving for the next big thing.

This insight shifted my perception of success.

Future wins weren't as emotionally fulfilling because happiness has a limit, and we naturally return to a baseline. I've come to see life as a heartbeat with inevitable ups and downs. Our goal is to minimize the extreme highs and lows. Once I understood that happiness follows this rhythm, my life changed. Now, I can finally step off the treadmill.

R: Restoration of motivation and wellness

Losing motivation, lacking clear goals, and constantly reinventing myself left me drained. My habit of "burning down my village" gave me no time to heal or find lasting motivation.

In a moment of deep reflection, I decided to prioritize my well-being. Creating a sanctuary at home became essential. I spent more quality time with my kids, doing activities they love, and set aside weekly date nights with my spouse to reconnect. Rebuilding family bonds became a priority; their love and support are integral to who I am. I began to understand the hidden dynamics of my life, and this led me to envision a lifestyle based on more than just chasing financial success. This book, my current venture, is fueled by how I want to live—not just by achievement or hard work.

Each day, my commitment strengthens. This journey isn't just about overcoming present struggles, but also preparing for what lies ahead. Healing past wounds, embracing the present, and shaping the future have become my focus. I've invested in holistic wellness, from body trackers to brain training systems, and prioritize genuine human connections over business commitments. Physical well-being, once neglected, now has the importance it deserves.

The next phase of my life isn't about chasing success but redefining it. I'm committed to shedding light on the emotional toll this journey takes and addressing the often-overlooked post-success blues. By speaking openly about my struggles, I hope to bring global awareness and empathy—much like how postpartum depression has been destigmatized. I'm ready to share my deepest wounds in hopes that someone will hear my story and know they're not alone.

These struggles are normal, and my goal is to equip high achievers with the tools they need to navigate their own journeys.

I've learned not to let my Success MNSTR consume me. Instead, I've named it, confronted it, and taken control.

To be continued...

Summary

In "The MNSTR Technique in Action," the focus is on real-life success stories that showcase the technique's practical application in overcoming challenges faced by high achievers. By following the MNSTR acronym, individuals gain insights into how mindset, neurochemical understanding, satisfaction, treadmill management, and restoration of wellness can transform struggles into growth opportunities. These stories demonstrate how high achievers manage setbacks, emotional lows, and burnout while applying the MNSTR Technique to regain control, balance, and motivation.

3 Key Takeaways:

1. **Real-Life Application:** The MNSTR Technique isn't one-size-fits-all, it's flexible. Use it as a practical framework to navigate personal and professional challenges by breaking down complex issues into manageable steps.

2. **Resilience through Stories:** Learn from the experiences of others who have successfully applied the MNSTR Technique to overcome obstacles and achieve lasting success.

3. **Sustain Progress:** Prioritize both achievement and well-being by balancing ambition with self-care, ensuring sustainable progress in all areas of life.

CHAPTER 11

Harnessing your MNSTR: The Power Within

Your private cheerleadcr

Defining your cheerleader

Naming your MNSTR triggers a unique neurological response, distinct from generic nouns. This name creates an emotional bond that deepens your relationship with your MNSTR, which is crucial to the process.

Understanding your MNSTR empowers you to take calculated risks, embrace change, explore new experiences, and command the attention of your peers.

Knowledge alone isn't power; actions shape your path. Your cheerleader is always in your corner, urging you forward. Recognize and name this supportive inner presence. Give it a place on the sidelines of your life, cheering you on through wins and losses.

Leveraging your cheerleader

The most significant personal growth often happens not in moments of peace, but in times of conflict and challenge. It's during moments of anger or frustration that you should practice harnessing your MNSTR, realizing you have choices in how you react and respond. Clarity, like seeing your reflection in calm water, emerges when you allow time for the boiling emotions to stop and sometimes, acknowledging that you are wrong can be just as powerful as being right.

Ignoring External Noise

You may have heard this story before, but it's worth sharing again for its powerful lesson. A woman approached her mentor and said, "I'm thinking about quitting the networking group."

He responded, "Can I ask why?"

She replied, "People seem constantly distracted. There's too much idle chatter, and no one seems truly committed. It feels like everyone is just pretending."

The mentor listened carefully and then said, "Before you make your decision, would you be willing to do a quick exercise for me?"

Curious, she agreed and asked, "What do you want me to do?"

He handed her a tray with several wine glasses filled to the brim and said, "I'd like you to walk around the room twice without spilling any wine."

She accepted the challenge and carefully completed the task.

"Done," she said.

The mentor then asked her three questions:

1. Did you notice anyone not paying attention?
2. Did you hear any gossip?
3. Did you see any signs of people lacking commitment?

She shook her head and said, "No, I didn't notice any of that. I was too focused on not spilling the wine."

The mentor smiled and said, "Exactly. When you're here, if you focus on your goals and contributions as intently as you did on those glasses, the distractions around you won't matter. Don't let others' disengagement influence your involvement. Concentrate on what you bring to the table and how you can grow. Now, imagine you're holding a glass of wine, and someone bumps into you, causing it to spill everywhere. Why did the wine spill?"

"Well, because someone bumped into me!" she said.

"But that's not the full story," said the mentor. "You spilled the wine because that's what was inside the glass. If it had been water, you would've spilled water. Whatever is in the glass is what will spill when it's shaken."

The same applies to life. When life shakes you—and it will—it's what's inside you that comes out. It's easy to keep things together until turbulence strikes.

So, ask yourself: What's in your cup?

When things get tough, what spills over? Is it joy, gratitude, peace, and humility? Or is it frustration, bitterness, and the urge to quit?

Life provides the cup, but you choose what fills it.

Let's focus on filling our cups with gratitude, resilience, positivity, kindness, and love, so that when life shakes us, the best of us pours out.

Understanding your **Success MNSTR Archetype** and using the **MNSTR Technique** to focus on what you can control is essential. This approach ensures you live your best life, keeping you grounded and motivated, no matter the distractions or pressures around you.

Fuel for your fire

Every action you take feeds a side of your MNSTR—the helpful or the hurtful—each with its own goals, challenges, and strategies. Which MNSTR is leading your journey?

Inside you, different aspects of your MNSTR often conflict. Achieving harmony within these inner dynamics requires daily self-awareness, especially when facing new challenges and victories. Use the free cellphone screensaver/wallpaper as a visual reminder to stay connected with your MNSTR. Every time you look at your phone, let it remind you of your Success MNSTR cheerleader and how to utilize its acronym—the technique.

You don't need to be extraordinary; consistent self-reflection, determination, and action are all you need to get what you want. Embracing failure builds the path to progress; with every setback, you're strengthening your resilience and exercising your failure muscle. Remember, one decision can change the trajectory of your life!

Summary

In "Harnessing Your MNSTR: The Power Within," the focus is on developing a personal bond with your Success MNSTR by giving it a unique name and role as your inner cheerleader. This chapter explains how recognizing your MNSTR helps manage emotions, especially during challenges, and encourages intentional focus on what you can control. It highlights tools like mindfulness, managing internal conflicts, and daily self-awareness as keys to fueling personal growth and resilience.

3 Key Takeaways:

1. **Name Your MNSTR**: Create a unique name for your MNSTR to establish a deeper emotional connection. This helps turn your internal motivator into a tangible ally during difficult moments.

2. **Focus on What You Control**: Practice staying focused on your goals and contributions, ignoring external distractions by concentrating on personal growth and self-improvement.

3. **Track and Reflect Daily**: Regular self-reflection helps you stay aligned with the MNSTR Technique, consistently feeding the side of your MNSTR that fuels your success and resilience,

CHAPTER 12

Navigating Your Cycles
of Sabotage or Comfort

Dig deeper beyond the surface... Step #3

As we conclude this journey, let's reflect on what true achievement means. Success isn't a straight path or a one-size-fits-all formula. It's marked by internal revelations, hard-won lessons, and deeper insights beyond surface-level accomplishments.

Now that you've identified and named your unique Success MNSTR Archetype persona(s) and you have the tools to master it using the MNSTR Technique acronym, the next step is to better understand your cycles of sabotage and comfort by taking the Success Paradox Self-Assessment.

The point of this self-assessment is to find out what cycles of sabotage are occurring in your mind and emotions immediately after you experience any form of accomplishment. Ironically, the immediate habit patterns and feelings that come up for us once we achieve any of our goals are the exact obstacles that then get in the way of us enjoying or repeating that same accomplishment in the future.

Light Side // Dark Side

Savor Success // Sabotage Success

Self-Awareness // Self-Doubt

Self-Clarity // Active Avoidance

Self-Expression // Censorship

Self-Release // Harsh Criticism

Taking the Success Paradox Self-Assessment

1. The Purpose and Benefits Behind the Assessment

This assessment provides an honest look at challenges you might face, such as perfectionism, lack of trust, fear of failure, imposter syndrome, the need for validation, never feeling happy, or not feeling "good enough", etc. Recognizing these sabotaging or comforting patterns is the third step to recovery and taking control of your next steps. So, "Now what?"

By identifying your sources of sabotage, you're taking the crucial step toward having total control over your individual journey. This assessment helps you understand your current position in the Success Paradox RIGHT NOW, revealing whether you are mostly sabotaging or comforting yourself. It highlights areas needing improvement to help you move forward more easily and quickly.

Use this information wisely, and you might never again have to ask, "Now what?"

2. The Process of the Assessment

This self-assessment is digitally accessible for your convenience and only takes a few minutes. Begin by returning to your saved free resources page or by scanning the QR code below with your phone to access the Success Paradox Self Assessment quiz. Follow the prompts and answer each question honestly to ensure the most accurate results. Remember, don't dwell on the questions and answers—move through them without over-evaluating yourself!

153

www.successmnstr.com/resources

Summary

In "Navigating Your Cycles of Sabotage or Comfort," the focus is on understanding your patterns of self-sabotage and comfort, particularly after achieving goals. Success MNSTR Archetypes help identify these behaviors through the Success Paradox Self-Assessment, allowing individuals to recognize mental and emotional cycles that hinder their growth. The chapter emphasizes personal accountability and self-reflection as crucial for maintaining balance and motivation after reaching milestones.

3 Key Takeaways:

1. **Identify Self-Sabotage Patterns:** Use the Success Paradox Self-Assessment to recognize behaviors that hinder growth and acknowledge recurring cycles of doubt and avoidance.

2. **Actively Address Comfort Zones:** Challenge habitual comfort patterns that prevent progress by setting adaptive goals and embracing discomfort as part of personal evolution.

3. **Reflect for Growth:** Regular self-reflection and honest assessment are essential to breaking limiting patterns and pushing toward meaningful, sustainable success.

Final Thoughts

Getting your shit together requires a level of honesty you can't even imagine until you're forced to confront it. There's nothing easy about realizing that you've been the one holding yourself back all along.

Success isn't just about reaching goals; it's about finding balance between achievement and inner fulfillment, knowing that today's peak will eventually become tomorrow's valley. You see this pattern over and over when people share their stories or in movies—the classic line, *"I have everything I ever wanted, but I'm still not happy."* That's their **Success MNSTR** talking. Or when someone says, *"I don't know who I am without my career, business, title, or sport,"* it's the same story. Whether it's the empty-nest parent who feels lost without their children, the caregiver who feels purposeless after their parents are gone, or someone who feels inferior or out of place—each of these moments reveals their **Success MNSTR** lurking in the background. The more you listen, the more you realize everyone is battling their own version of it.

Take Simone Biles, for example. Society was quick to label her weak, a quitter, even a disgrace to her team and country. But her return wasn't about reclaiming titles—it was about being true to herself: Success should never come at the expense of your health. True greatness shines when you honor your well-being—physically, mentally, and emotionally. Whether she realized it or not, Simone identified her Success MNSTR and took control of it using the MNSTR Technique showcased in her Netflix docuseries, with the kind of courage the world rarely sees. (I'll say it because that's how I see it—though it would be incredible to hear her thoughts on it!) In a world that's crying out for authentic role models, Simone became exactly that. She's the kind of hero I want my children to look up to.

Then there's Stephen Nedoroscik—he didn't follow the usual path to success, but his unwavering support for his teammates and relentless focus on a single discipline (a rarity in this sport) as a pommel horse specialist earned him two Olympic bronze medals. Like Simone, he recognized which MNSTR to feed and found the delicate balance between dedication and ambition, ultimately carving out his own version of success.

His journey reminds us that success isn't a one-size-fits-all concept. There's no single blueprint for finding your purpose or success. Embrace every part of who you are, without apology, and you'll discover you've been the hero of your own story all along. True growth comes from the struggles you face, the honesty in your reflection, and the deep conversations you have with yourself.

As you navigate your own path, never forget that everyone will try to paint a picture of what your life should look like, but only you hold the brush. You decide whether to follow their vision or create your own masterpiece. In the realm of mental health, no two journeys are the same, and it's up to you to decide how you'll rise.

When you think about your next steps, remember this: transformation begins the moment you take action. Whether you start with the assessments in this book, use the Success MNSTR Workbook, or share your insights with someone close to you, each step brings you closer to meaningful change.

My hope is for everyone to understand that feeling a sense of letdown, blues, or even depression after accomplishing a goal is part of the process. The bigger the goal, the bigger the depression. Don't expect to feel happy or satisfied indefinitely—allow yourself the rhythm of a heartbeat and give yourself permission to fail. Acknowledge this, offer yourself space and grace, and then when you're ready, push forward once again.

Commit to your growth, and the universe will conspire to support you. But if you ever feel the footsteps of your **Success MNSTR** creeping up on you, remember to chant:

"MINDSET.
NEUROCHEMICAL.
SATISFACTION.
TREADMILL.
RESTORATION."

Recognize your relationship with these principles, and use the tools you now have to tame your own Success MNSTR.

THANK YOU FOR READING MY BOOK!

To access your free bonuses, head back to the bookmarked resource page from the QR code at the start of the book, check your email, or simply re-scan the code with your phone. Trust me, you'll want to claim your gift—I use mine every day!

Scan the QR Code with your Phone Here:

www.successmnstr.com/resources

I appreciate your interest in my book and value your feedback as it helps me improve future versions of this book. I would appreciate it if you could leave your invaluable review on Amazon.com with your feedback. Thank you!

References

1. Journal Neuron https://www.cell.com/neuron/fulltext/S0896-6273%2816%2930157-X

2. Study by Deloitte in 2015, 77% of the population grapple with burnout https://www2.deloitte.com/us/en/pages/about-deloitte/articles/burnout-survey.html

3. World Health Organization (WHO) in 2022, 15% of working-age adults were estimated to have a mental disorder in 2019 https://www.who.int/newsroom/fact-sheets/detail/mental-health-at-work

4. WHO: 1 in 8 people - mental disorders https://www.who.int/news-room/fact-sheets/detail/mental-disorders

5. Marist Institute: income $50,000 (great graphics) https://maristpoll.marist.edu/wp-content/misc/Home%20instead/Money%20Matters_April%202012_FINAL.pdf

6. False hope syndrome https://psycnet.apa.org/doiLanding?doi=10.1037%2F0003-066X.57.9.677

7. Roger Bannister broke the record for running a four-minute mile https://en.wikipedia.org/wiki/Four-minute_mile#:~=The%20four%2Dminute%20barrier%20was,and%20Chris%20Brasher%20as%20pacemakers

8. Recent discoveries highlight the brain's remarkable adaptability at every stage of life https://www.nature.com/articles/nature25975.epdf?sharing_token=sYQoTgx5zhKuPKUgo0z_n9RgN0jAjWel9jnR3ZoTv0O2r5tZrKCowVRghD0l8MzB8APs774yJ9j3Od4E7EqgO_T8vvqRcnX8V0gLEcSgyWJeltr9J

Z_qMs-
bOZ3N9NM3MRQNDTxFn_cRTxQuH7I5tO_yIiRNNggZ8TL8hfJrnznv3jRb1
uDMTaAtwcxrdd2TMKr-
SuMHsk2KW2BD66GkfmA%3D%3D&tracking_referrer=www.statnews.com

9. Dr. Carol Dweck, who is the Lewis and Virginia Eaton Professor of Psychology at Stanford University https://www.edutopia.org/profile/carol-dweck/#:~=Carol%20S.,how%20to%20foster%20their%20success and https://en.wikipedia.org/wiki/Carol_Dweck

10. The Notorious B.I.G. once said, "Mo money, mo problems" https://en.wikipedia.org/wiki/Mo_Money_Mo_Problems

11. NASA's studies on naps https://www.sleepfoundation.org/sleep-hygiene/nasa-nap#:~=The%20original%201995%20NASA%20study,those%20who%20didn't%20nap

12. Steve Jobs, 1996 PBS documentary Triumph of the Nerds https://www.pbs.org/nerds/part1.html

13. Gene variants may be linked to our overall happiness levels https://www.news-medical.net/news/20231015/Is-your-happiness-hardwired-New-study-dives-into-the-genetics-of-joy.aspx#:~=Study%20findings&text=The%20genetic%20predisposition%20of%20happiness,to%20psychological%20and%20cognitive%20health

14. Dopamine https://www.ncbi.nlm.nih.gov/pmc/articles/PMC4684895/#:~=Dopamine%20is%20a%20neurotransmitter%20that,in%20different%20nervous%20system%20diseases

15. Serotonin https://www.ncbi.nlm.nih.gov/pmc/articles/PMC5864293/#:~=In%20the%20central%20nervous%20system,system%20in%20the%20human%20brain

16. Norepinephrine https://my.clevelandclinic.org/health/articles/22610-norepinephrine-noradrenaline

17. Endorphins https://my.clevelandclinic.org/health/body/23040-endorphins

18. Oxytocin https://www.health.harvard.edu/mind-and-mood/oxytocin-the-love-hormone

19. HUG https://www.medicinenet.com/how_do_hugs_make_you_feel/article.htm

20. Harvard Professor Arthur Brooks: having more money didn't help them become happier https://arthurbrooks.com/

21. Why Success Doesn't Lead to Satisfaction https://hbr.org/2023/01/why-success-doesnt-lead-to-satisfaction

22. Wendy Wood, PhD, a psychologist at the University of Southern California (USC) https://www.apa.org/monitor/2020/11/career-lab-habits

23. Habit and Identity https://www.frontiersin.org/journals/psychology/articles/10.3389/fpsyg

Printed in the USA
CPSIA information can be obtained
at www.ICGtesting.com
CBHW052031241024
16329CB00006B/72/J